MACMILLAN ACADEMIC SKILLS

Skillful

Reading&Writing

Student's Book

3

Authors: Jennifer Bixby & Jaimie Scanlon
Series Consultant: Dorothy E. Zemach

Cont

Grammar	Writing skill	Writing task	Digibook video activity	Study skills
Clause joining with subordinators	Paragraph structure	A paragraph about your identity	Shared identity	Am I a smart reader?
Non-defining relative clauses	Transitions: introducing opposing ideas	The pros and cons of a design	The counterfeit wars	Editing and proofreading strategies
Adverb clauses of reason and purpose	Summarizing	A summary and a response paragraph	Thought development	Plagiarism
Adverbs as stance markers	Using sensory details in a narrative	Narrative essay: A time when you faced danger	Fire and fun	Managing stress
Object noun clauses with *that*	Using sentence variety	Response to an exam question	Our journey, our dreams	Strategies for writing timed essays
Passive modals: advice, ability, and possibility	Thesis statements	Persuasive essay: A health recommendation	Pills	Participating in online discussion boards
Unreal conditional in the past	Writing about cause and effect	Describing a challenging situation	Adaptation	Using desired outcomes to guide study strategy
Intensifier + comparative combinations	Effective hooks	A proposal	Profiles of success	Selecting and evaluating online sources
Cleft sentences with *what*	Using similes and metaphors	A descriptive anecdote	Communication	Using the thesaurus
The future progressive	Qualifying statistical data	A report on a current trend	Future friends	Developing a portfolio

To the Student

Academic success requires so much more than memorizing facts. It takes skills. This means that a successful student can both learn and think critically.

Skillful gives you:

- Skills for learning about a wide variety of topics from different angles and from different academic areas
- Skills you need to succeed when reading and listening to these texts
- Skills you need to succeed when writing for and speaking to different audiences
- Skills for critically examining the issues presented by a speaker or a writer
- Study skills for learning and remembering the English language and important information.

To successfully use this book, use these strategies:

- **Come to class prepared to learn** This means that you should show up well-fed, well-rested, and prepared with the proper materials (paper, pen, textbook, completed homework, and so on).
- **Ask questions and interact** Learning a language is not passive. You need to actively participate. Help your classmates, and let them help you. It is easier to learn a language with other people.
- **Practice** Do each exercise a few times, with different partners. Memorize and use new language. Use the *Skillful* Digibook to develop the skills presented in the Student's Book. Complete the additional activities on your computer outside of class to make even more progress.
- **Review your work** Look over the the skills, grammar, and vocabulary from previous units. Study a little bit each day, not just before tests.
- **Be an independent learner, too** Look for opportunities to study and practice English outside of class, such as reading for pleasure and using the Internet in English. Find and then share information about the different unit topics with your classmates.

Remember that learning skills, like learning a language, takes time and practice. Be patient with yourself, but do not forget to set goals. Check your progress and be proud of your success!

I hope you enjoy using *Skillful*!

Dorothy E. Zemach
Series Consultant

Welcome to *Skillful*!

Each *Skillful* unit has ten pages and is divided into two main sections: reading skills and writing skills.

Reading

The reading skills section always comes first and starts with a *Discussion point* to lead you in to the unit topic.

There are then two reading texts for you to practice your reading skills on. There are activities to practice your global reading skills and your close reading skills, as well as opportunities to critically examine the ideas in the texts. Key academic vocabulary from the text is presented on the page so you can see essential terms to learn.

Vocabulary skills also give you the chance to develop the ways in which you learn and remember vocabulary from the reading texts.

Writing

The writing section has two main parts: grammar and writing skills. You can find information on each of these in boxes on the page and these give essential information on these skills. At the end of this section is a writing task for you to put the ideas from the texts and the skills from the writing section into practice. Use the checklist on page 109 to see how well your partner has completed the task.

The final page in the unit focuses on study skills which will help you to achieve academic success. Some of these pages come from *The Study Skills Handbook* by Stella Cottrell, while others are engaging scenarios for you to read and reflect on.

Using *Skillful* gives you everything you need for academic success.

Good luck!

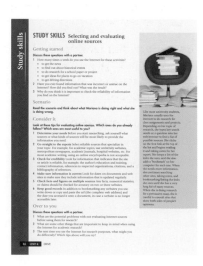

Introduction

Each *Skillful* Student's Book comes with a code in the back of the book that gives you free access to the accompanying Digibook. The Digibook encourages a more interactive and engaging learning environment and is very simple to access. Just go to www.skillfuldigibooks.com, and follow the step-by-step instructions to get started!

The first time you access the Digibook you will need an Internet connection, but after this it is possible to work offline if you wish.

Digital Student's Book

This contains all the same content as your printed Student's Book, but you can use it on your computer, enabling easier navigation through the pages, a zoom function to create better student focus, and a personal annotation resource for helpful classroom notes.

Skillful Practice

You can either complete the extra activities as you go through the Digital Student's Book via the interactive icons, or you can find them all in one place in the *Skillful* Practice area. Here you will find a variety of activities to practice all the new skills and language you have learned in the Student's Book, including vocabulary, grammar, and skills-based activities.

There are also additional productive tasks and video activities linked to the unit topics.

If you complete any of the extra activities while you are online, your score will be recorded in your markbook so that your teacher can track your progress. If you work offline your scores will be stored and transferred to your markbook the next time you connect.

Whether online or offline, in the classroom or on the move, the *Skillful* Digibook allows you to access and use its content while encouraging interactive learning and effortless self-study.

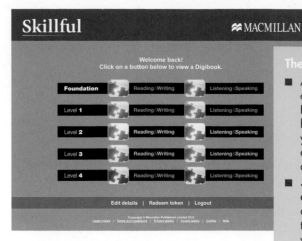

The Digibook contains:

- A digital version of the Student's Book, complete with hotspots that take you to embedded audio and other additional content;
- *Skillful* Practice, with extra interactive activities for you to review what you have learned, including video-based activities.

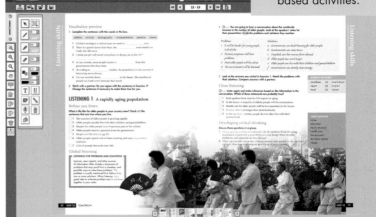

The Digital Student's Book also contains lots of hotspots that link to additional content not in your printed Student's Book:

- Audio files for all of the reading texts
- Useful language to support discussion activities
- Dictionary definitions for the *Academic Keywords*
- Unit checklists so you can monitor how well you are progressing through the course.

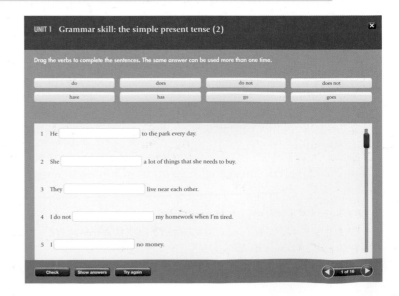

Identity

READING	Previewing
	Understanding key terms
	Identifying the main idea
VOCABULARY	Choosing the right word form
WRITING	Paragraph structure
GRAMMAR	Clause joining with subordinators

Discussion point

Discuss these questions with a partner.

1 What are five words that you would use to answer the question 'Who are you?'
2 What are some of the social groups you belong to?
3 In what ways are these groups important to you? Explain your answers.

Vocabulary preview

Match the words with the correct definitions.

1 improve or strengthen (e.g. skills, abilities)   ___   **a** aspect
2 a particular part, feature, or quality of something   ___   **b** connect with
3 ideas that explain something   ___   **c** consist of
4 to be made of particular parts or things   ___   **d** core
5 to feel you understand someone   ___   **e** develop
6 to show the existence or nature of something   ___   **f** rediscover
7 to find something that has been lost   ___   **g** reflect
8 the most important or basic part of something   ___   **h** theory

READING 1 Discuss it online

Before you read

PREVIEWING

Quickly previewing a text before you read is a good way to improve your reading comprehension. Ask yourself these questions before you read.

- Look at the title, subtitle, and headings (or sections). Look at any photos and captions. What do you think the article will be about? Where would you read this type of article (e.g. in a textbook, in a newspaper)?
- What type of article is it?
- Who is the intended audience?
- What can you learn from this article?

Preview *Discuss it online* **by answering the questions in the skill box. Then discuss your answers with a partner.**

Global reading

Read *Discuss it online* **and answer the questions.**

1 Why did the instructor ask students to answer the question before the lecture?
2 What happened in high school that changed Ali's identity?
3 What are some values that Ali writes about?
4 Why was high school a difficult time for Paul?
5 How did choosing different friends change Paul's life?
6 Paul says, 'Your chosen identity is not who you are.' Would Ali agree?

Close reading

UNDERSTANDING KEY TERMS

In academic texts, key terms are often described using a definition, an example, or an explanation. When you come across a key term, look at the text before or after it to see how it is defined. Then underline or highlight the key term. You may want to write it in your notebook with your own definition for it. Connecting a key term to your own life will help you remember it.

Read *Discuss it online* again and answer the questions.

1 What key terms are defined by the instructor?
2 What information is given to help you understand the terms?
3 According to definitions given, what type of identity is 'soccer player' for Ali: given, chosen, or core identity?
4 Fill in the circles on the right with examples from your own identity. Write three examples in each circle.

Given identity	Chosen identity	Core identity
◯	◯	◯

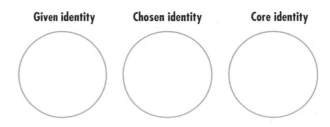

DISCUSS IT ONLINE [BLOG] [DISCUSSION]
Discussion Board, Intro to Psychology 101, Fall semester

Ungraded question, posted by Instructor, Dr. Green.
In next week's lecture, we will be discussing identity. Social psychologists suggest that we have three basic types of identity. First, your given identity includes your gender, your birthplace, and your age. These are aspects of identity that are almost impossible to change. Second is your chosen identity, groups you choose to become a part of. Chosen identity can include your religion, your political beliefs, your career, or your community organizations. Finally, your core identity is what makes you unique. Your behaviors, personality, values, and skills are all part of your core identity. Before Monday's lecture, post a short reply to this question.

QUESTION: How has your identity changed in the last few years? Include reference to the three aspects of identity.

Posted by Ali K.
When I started high school, I thought that I knew exactly who I was and where I was headed. I was a star soccer player, and my entire identity was soccer — I lived it and breathed it. This was my chosen identity. Everything changed when I had a terrible knee injury during my second year. After several months, it was clear that I wouldn't be able to play soccer competitively again. I was devastated when I had to quit the team, and I was depressed. Gradually, I started to see that I was still the same person on the inside. I was still a very hard-working person, someone who didn't easily give up, and someone who loved being on a team. These were part of my core identity. I had to rediscover my values (hard work and competition) to get me through this hard time. I've been developing a new sense of identity. Although I've had to change part of my chosen identity, I now understand that my core identity (who I am inside) is the most important for me.

Posted by Paul S.
Like Ali, I had a very rough time in high school. I felt like my parents didn't understand or respect me, and nothing I did was right in their eyes. They didn't think I was trustworthy, and I admit that sometimes I didn't make great choices. But my parents are part of my given identity, and therefore they are very important in my life. During high school, my chosen identity was the group of friends that I belonged to. However, some friends were influencing me in bad ways. I felt really lost and unhappy with my life. Later, when I started at the university in my city, I decided to find some new friends. I've connected with friends who better understand my family background and my values. Now I feel more comfortable around my parents because they respect me as an adult. It is important to remember that your chosen identity is not who you are. You can make other choices, and change your life.

Developing critical thinking

Discuss these questions in a group.

1 If you had to write a response to the discussion board question, what part of your identity would you write about? Why?
2 Why is the family an important part of a person's identity?

ACADEMIC KEYWORDS

influence	(v)	/ˈɪnfluəns/
respect	(v)	/rɪˈspekt/
values	(n)	/ˈvæljuz/

READING 2 Sports fans and identity

Before you read

Discuss these questions in a group.

1 Which sports are the most popular with sports fans where you live?
2 What are some characteristics of a sports fan?
3 Think of a friend or relative who is a sports fan. Why do you think this person loves sports?

Global reading

USEFUL LANGUAGE
committed
enthusiastic
loyal
optimistic

IDENTIFYING THE MAIN IDEA

Identifying the main idea of each paragraph is a good way to check your comprehension. You can find the main idea after you read each paragraph or as you read the text a second time. Either highlight or underline the information, or make a short note in the margin.

Read the main idea statements below. Then skim *Sports fans and identity* and write the paragraph number next to each idea. Mark the statement you don't need with an *X*.

___ **a** People want others to think highly of the group they belong to.

___ **b** Fans of a winning team feel more self-confident and are more likely to spend money.

___ **c** Sports fans often feel like they have thousands of friends.

___ **d** By studying language, we can see that fans feel closer to the team when it is winning.

___ **e** Sports fans include many different types of people, but they are all part of a special group.

___ **f** Social identity theory is about how we categorize people in groups, and how we identify with certain groups more than others.

Close reading

1 **Find the terms in bold in *Sports fans and identity*. Then complete the sentences to define the terms.**

   1 **Individual identity** consists of _____.

   2 According to **social identity theory**, _____.

   3 **Self-esteem** means _____.

2 **Read the sentences about *Sports fans and identity*. Write *T* (True) or *F* (False). Then correct the false statements.**

   1 Most sports fans feel connected with other fans of the same team. ___

   2 The groups we belong to do not influence our self-esteem. ___

   3 Henri Tajfel and John Turner wrote about core identity in sports. ___

   4 Researchers found that fans use different nouns to talk about their team, depending on if the team won or lost. ___

   5 Winning a championship can have an effect on the self-confidence of fans. ___

SPORTS FANS AND IDENTITY

[1] Each of us knows someone who is crazy about a particular sports team. Perhaps we are sports fans, too. Sports attract fans from all walks of life: students, senior citizens, truck drivers, and bankers. Being a sports fan instantly connects you to a very large community of people who have a common passion. Some fans say that when you walk into a sports stadium, you instantly feel that you have thousands of friends. You belong to a very special group of people, and when your team wins, you feel great. Sports fans seem to connect their own identity to their chosen team and feel connected with the team and players.

[2] Our individual identity consists of many things, including our gender, personality, abilities, and social groups. The groups we choose to belong to, from community groups to groups of sports fans, shape our identity. Related to this is the social identity theory, developed in 1979 by Henri Tajfel and John Turner. They suggested that we naturally categorize people into groups. For example, we categorize people by gender (male, female), by profession (dentist, lawyer), or by nationality (British, Japanese). In defining who we are, we may more closely identify with our professional group (I am a software engineer) than with our gender group (I am a man or woman). We also decide which groups we belong to, based on different aspects of our identity. According to the social identity theory, our self-esteem — how we feel about ourselves — is reflected in the groups we choose to belong to.

[3] This theory says that since our self-esteem is related to belonging to certain groups, we want our group to be seen more positively than other groups. For instance, if you identify strongly with your favorite sports team, you want to believe that your team is better than other teams. According to social identity theory, we naturally protect the groups that we identify with and belong to, while devaluing other groups. We speak well and think highly of the team we support, while we may make negative comments about an opposing team.

[4] Two interesting studies point out the unique connection between sports and identity. First, researchers have studied language used by sports fans to talk about their teams. Dr. Robert Cialdini, a professor and well-known expert on the psychology of influence, showed that when teams did well, fans would closely identify themselves with the team. For example, by using pronouns like 'we', fans show that they feel closely connected with the team when it is winning. 'We really killed that team. They couldn't get the ball past us. Did you see our last play?' However, when teams didn't do well, fans would distance themselves from the losing team, using different pronouns. 'They didn't know what they were doing. They had no strategy.'

[5] Social scientists have also studied the effect of winning a national football championship in the U.S. on the fans of the winning team. They have found that fans have more self-confidence and feel more competent, probably because team victories reflect well on their personal sense of identity. When people feel more competent, they perform better at work and are likely to earn and spend more money (Coats and Humphreys, 2002, *The economic impact of postseason play in professional sports*). Experts say that for these reasons, it is likely that a winning team may have a positive influence on the economy of a city.

Developing critical thinking

1 Answer the questions. Then discuss them in a group.

1 Read each statement based on *Sports fans and identity*. Then mark if you agree (✓), disagree (✗), or if you are not sure (NS). Think of a comment or example to explain your answer.

  1 When you are a fan of a particular team, at a game or event, you instantly feel that you have thousands of friends. ___

  2 If a sports team is a very important part of a fan's identify, winning is extremely important. ___

  3 Winning a championship changes the way the fans feel about themselves for a short time. ___

2 Why do you think fans continue to support a team that does poorly year after year?

ACADEMIC KEYWORDS		
identify	(v)	/aɪˈdentɪˌfaɪ/
perform	(v)	/pərˈfɔrm/
individual	(adj)	/ˌɪndɪˈvɪdʒuəl/

2 Think about the ideas from *Discuss it online* and *Sports fans and identity*. Discuss these questions in a group.

1 What is your most important chosen or group identity? Why?

2 Do you think that most people are more interested in being unique or belonging to a group? Explain why.

Vocabulary skill

CHOOSING THE RIGHT WORD FORM

Recognizing common word forms and knowing how words change for different parts of speech will increase your writing accuracy and your vocabulary.

Sometimes, words that may seem the same can have different meanings. A *confidant* (n) (someone you can trust and discuss private feelings with) is quite different from *confident* (adj) (describing someone who believes in their own abilities).

USEFUL LANGUAGE
be a fan
belong to a group
be unique
family background
feel a connection
values

1 Complete the chart. Use a dictionary to check. Then choose the correct words to complete the sentences. Change the form if necessary.

Noun	Verb	Adjective
	choose	
concern		
identity		
struggle		
		trustworthy

1 My team's fans are _____ by their green and gold clothing.

2 If your test scores are very high, you will have more _____ of where to attend college.

3 Yesterday my instructor _____ me to give the first presentation.

4 When Tran first moved to Los Angeles, he was very _____ about housing and transportation.

5 It's important to have _____ friends, at all stages of our lives.

6 My brother is very shy and _____ with social situations.

2 Correct the questions. Then discuss them with a partner.

1 What are you concern about at the moment?

2 Do you have more confident with reading or listening?

3 Do you find it easy to make chooses?

WRITING A paragraph about your identity

You are going to learn about writing clear paragraphs with topic sentences, supporting sentences, and concluding sentences. You are also going to learn about joining clauses with subordinators and write a paragraph about your identity.

Writing skill

PARAGRAPH STRUCTURE

When you write a paragraph, you want your main idea to be clear and you want the reader to understand your point of view.

Topic sentences

Use a clear **topic sentence** at the beginning of each paragraph to help readers identify your topic and your idea or opinion about it. The topic sentence is often, but not always, the first sentence.

Supporting sentences

The body of a paragraph consists of **supporting sentences**. These sentences must connect to the topic and support the main idea.

Concluding sentences

A **concluding sentence** restates the topic sentence or connects back to it. Not all paragraphs have a clear concluding sentence.

Clear organization will help your reader navigate your paragraph. You can either use:

*   **listing** organization: listing several points to support a main idea, or
*   **time order** organization, using the sequence of events.

1 **Re-read paragraphs 1 and 2 in *Discuss it online* and answer the questions.**

  1 Paragraph 1
  a Write the topic sentence.
  b How many points does the paragraph make?
  c Does the paragraph use listing organization or time order organization?
  d Does it have a concluding sentence that restates the topic sentence?

  2 Paragraph 2
  a Write the topic sentence.
  b Does the paragraph use listing organization or time order organization?
  c Does it have a concluding sentence that connects back to the topic sentence?

2 **Read each topic sentence. Then list three points to support the sentence. Use listing organization.**

  1 At our school, students can be divided into three main types.

  a _____
  b _____
  c _____

  2 For me, a friend needs three important characteristics.

  a _____
  b _____
  c _____

  3 Although I may seem like an average person, I have three unique abilities.

  a _____
  b _____
  c _____

Grammar

CLAUSE JOINING WITH SUBORDINATORS

When you join two clauses together with a subordinating conjunction, you have a sentence with a dependent clause and an independent clause. Here are some common subordinating conjunctions: *because, since, when, after, before, until, as soon as, although, even though, if, where.*

dependent clause   *independent clause*

When I started high school, I was very shy.

independent clause   *dependent clause*

I was very shy **because I was new to the school**.

Watch for these common writing errors:

* Joining two sentences with a comma:

  My brother and I are alike in many aspects, we look entirely different.

  *My brother and I are alike in many aspects, **although** we look entirely different.*

* Using a dependent clause without an independent clause:

  Whenever I am concerned about the project.

  *Whenever I am concerned about the project, **I call my advisor.***

1 **For each sentence, cross out the <u>one</u> subordinating conjunction that does <u>not</u> work.**

  1 I will be finished with my homework **before / after / as soon as** I figure out this math problem.

  2 **Before / Because / Since** there had been many injuries at the beginning of the game, the team struggled during the second half.

  3 **Since / Although / Whenever** she was eighteen, her parents were the ones who chose the university she would attend.

  4 The police were contacted **although / when / as soon as** the community realized that pedestrians were in danger at the intersection.

  5 I realized my mistake with the recipe **if / before / after** I put the cake in the oven.

  6 **When / Even though / If** students understand the core values of a school, they begin to show more respect for differences.

2 **Read each sentence and mark if it is correct (✓) or incorrect (✗). Then make corrections.**

  1 Because I didn't understand the theory in physics class.   ____

  2 I had many struggles during my first semester, the second semester seemed much easier.   ____

  3 He didn't have much self-confidence, he had failed the course twice already.   ____

  4 As long as I do homework for several hours every night, I won't get behind.   ____

  5 Even though she was extremely beautiful.   ____

  6 Their favorite coach is fired the fans will be very upset.   ____

WRITING TASK

Write a paragraph describing the different types of your own identity.

Audience: teacher
Context: personal reflection on a text
Purpose: to relate course material to personal life

BRAINSTORM

1 Read the model paragraph about identity. Find the topic sentence and the concluding sentence. Circle the subordinating coordinator that joins two independent clauses. Don't complete the model yet.

> There are three different aspects that define my identity: my _____ identity, _____ identity, and _____ identity. My given identity is made up of facts. For example, I am _____. My chosen identity consists of groups that I have chosen to belong to. For example, _____. I enjoy these groups because _____. My core identity is made up of my abilities and characteristics. Some of my unique abilities are _____. My characteristics are that I am _____. Of the three aspects of identity, for me my _____ identity is the most important right now.

2 Look back at the circles you filled in on page 9. Draw three more circles on a page. Fill them in with more ideas for each identity type, adding new words and phrases.

PLAN

Answer these questions to expand your ideas for writing.

1 Do you have at least three examples for each type of identity? If not, add more examples.
2 For each type of identity, what is the most important aspect for you? Why?
    a given identity
    b chosen identity
    c core identity
3 Which type of identity has become more important to you recently? Why?

WRITE

Write your paragraph. You can use the model as a guide, or write independently. Make sure your paragraph has a topic and concluding sentence, and support for your ideas. Join some clauses with subordinating conjunctions to connect ideas.

SHARE

Exchange paragraphs with a partner. Read the checklist on page 109 and provide feedback to your partner.

REWRITE AND EDIT

Consider your partner's comments and write a final draft.

Am I a smart reader?

by Stella Cottrell

Know exactly what you are looking for

☐ Do I know what questions I'm trying to answer?
☐ Have I considered what information I need?

Use reading lists selectively

☐ Have I looked at the recommended reading list?
☐ Do I know what I need to read?

Examine sources for suitability

☐ Have I considered each source? Have I considered:
  - whether it's on the reading list?
  - whether it's up-to-date or not?
  - whether it looks readable?
  - whether it has the information I want?

Find information quickly

☐ Have I tried using an index?
☐ Have I got faster with practice?

Select relevant parts of the book

☐ Do I browse the book quickly?
☐ Do I use the contents page, the index, the headings, and the subheadings for guidance?
☐ Do I identify which parts of which chapters I need, and put markers in these?

Select relevant parts of the page

☐ Do I read the chapter heading?
☐ Do I read any subheadings?
☐ Do I read the first sentence of each paragraph (which should introduce the topic summaries or conclusions)?

Use photocopies

☐ Do I use marker pens to highlight important words and phrases (only)?
☐ Do I note ideas and thoughts in the margins?
☐ Do I make notes about the points I highlighted, to help me remember them?

Chart the main ideas

☐ Do I map out ideas so that I can see how everything fits together?

Practice second-guessing

☐ Do I keep trying to anticipate what is coming next, or what the conclusions will be?

Using large photocopies

- For an important diagram or map, make an enlarged photocopy. Attach it to a large poster.
- As you read, photocopy short key passages. Reduce them in size and attach them to the poster.
- Link ideas using color and arrows. Add your own notes.

These posters are very useful for revision.

Read interactively

☐ Do I question what I'm reading?
☐ Do I look for answers to my questions?
☐ Do I make notes of the important points, and ideas generated by what I read?
☐ Do I challenge the assumptions of the writer, the logic of the arguments, and the validity of the conclusions?

Vary reading speed and method

☐ Do I keep changing the pace, according to the needs of the text?
☐ Do I scan rapidly for specific information?
☐ Do I read quickly to get the general sense of a passage, and then read difficult parts slowly?

Design

READING	Scanning
	Recognizing cause and effect
VOCABULARY	Prefix *over-*
WRITING	Transitions: introducing opposing ideas
GRAMMAR	Non-defining relative clauses

Discussion point

Discuss these questions with a partner.

1 Look at the picture above. Do you know where it is? What makes it special? What do you like or dislike about the way it is designed?

2 Think of three other famous buildings or structures from around the world that you feel are well designed. What makes them interesting or beautiful?

3 Choose a famous building or structure from your country. What do you like about its design? What do you dislike?

Vocabulary preview

Complete the passage with the words in the box.

> construction   devise   dilemma   eyesore   feat   iconic
> landmarks   opponents   priority

Known around the world as the symbol of Paris, France, the Eiffel Tower is one of the world's most (1) _____ structures. When the tower was built in the late 1800s, it was truly an amazing (2) _____ of engineering and design. The tower was designed by two French engineers working under Gustave Eiffel. Their assignment was to (3) _____ a plan for a centerpiece structure for the 1889 Exposition Universelle, a World's Fair which would be hosted in Paris. When Eiffel presented the final design to the Exposition planners, he found he had a (4) _____. A group of Parisian architects, artists, and others concerned with the city's image called the tower an (5) _____. These (6) _____ felt that the tower would 'crush' the beauty of Paris's traditional (7) _____, such as Notre Dame Cathedral, and the Arc de Triomphe. Eiffel fought back assuring the group that keeping the city's beautiful image was also a (8) _____ for him. His response worked. (9) _____ of the tower was completed in March of 1889. The design of the tower amazed the public at the 1889 Exposition, and continues to delight visitors to Paris from around the world.

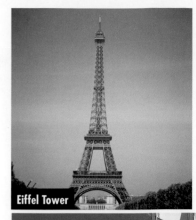

Eiffel Tower

READING 1   The Metropol Parasol

Before you read

Work with a partner. Think of an open area in or near your town. If you could design and build anything you wanted there, what would it be?

Global reading

1 **What is the Metropol Parasol? Read the article, then discuss your answer with a partner.**

> **SCANNING**
>
> Scanning is looking quickly through a text to locate specific information (e.g. a word in a dictionary, a fact in an article). When you scan, move your eyes quickly over the text. Focus on what you are looking for and search for key words. What to look out for:
>
> - <u>dates and times</u>: scan for **numbers** (*1972, 8:30*)
> - <u>names of people or places</u>: scan for **capital letters** (*New York*)
> - <u>a sequence of events</u>: scan for **numbers** and **signal words** (*First, Secondly*)
> - <u>ideas, opinions, or examples</u>: scan for **signal words** and **phrases** (*However, In other words, In addition, For example, such as*)
> - <u>organization cues</u> such as **italicized** and **bold words**.

2 **Read the following questions about *The Metropol Parasol*. What kinds of information should you look for?**

1 Where is the Metropol Parasol?
2 Who designed the structure?
3 How long did it take to build?
4 How much did it cost?
5 What is on the upper level?

3 **Scan *The Metropol Parasol* and write the answers to the questions.**

Close reading

Read the sentences about *The Metropol Parasol*. Write *T* (True) or *F* (False). Then correct the false statements.

1 The construction site was originally planned as a gas station. ___
2 The buildings are raised off the ground to protect the ruins below. ___
3 The structure was designed to be a museum, a shopping center, and a meeting place. ___
4 Some people feel that it shows Seville is becoming more modern. ___
5 Opponents say the design isn't appropriate for Seville. ___

The Metropol Parasol

¹ While beginning construction on a new parking garage in 2003, workers in Seville, Spain were suddenly faced with a dilemma. The garage's construction site was right on top of a large area of ancient Roman ruins. Seville city officials knew that preserving these priceless treasures from ancient history was far more important to their city than adding a few parking spaces. The mayor stopped construction immediately, and the city devised a new plan for the space.

² After many long meetings, officials finally reached a decision. They would convert the space into a museum where visitors from near and far could view the artifacts. But they didn't want just another building. They felt that the center of Seville needed an inviting community center, where people could meet friends, sit outdoors and read a book, shop, eat in restaurants, and just enjoy themselves. They wanted it to be spacious and open, but also to provide shade against Seville's hot summer sun — part museum, part mall, and part city square. But what would it look like? And how could they build there without disturbing the Roman ruins? To select the design, the city held a competition for architects around the world. The aim was to create a unique structure that would protect the ruins while also creating a lively, open public space. After reviewing hundreds of applications from around the world, the judges settled on a design by Jürgen Mayer H., who is a German architect. Mayer called his design the *Metropol Parasol*.

³ Building the parasol was no easy feat. Protecting the Roman ruins was a priority. As a result, workers were not allowed to dig large areas of the ground. Instead, the parasol was designed to 'float' above the ground. In fact, in an area covering 18,000 square meters, the four-storey, 29 meter-high structure only touches the ground in six places! With this unusual design, safety had to be considered very carefully. The wooden exterior was put in place over a super strong frame of concrete, steel, and granite. Building took seven years and cost 90 million euros to complete. Today the parasol complex houses an underground archeological museum, a farmer's market, and many cafés and restaurants. On the upper level, visitors can enjoy views of Seville from the panorama deck.

⁴ So, how will the Metropol Parasol influence future city planning and architectural design? As with any element of design, the Parasol is attracting differing opinions. Some say the structure is an iconic landmark and a work of art — a sign that Seville is changing with the times. Opponents call it an overpriced eyesore and say the odd mushroom shape doesn't fit with the rest of the city. Others, who are looking at it from an ecological viewpoint, wish the city had just planted more trees instead of using all that wood. Are the critics overreacting? Will these kinds of manufactured landscapes be the way of the future? We'll have to wait and see.

Developing critical thinking

Discuss these questions in a group.

1 Consider the different opinions about the Metropol Parasol. What do you think? Make a list of the advantages and disadvantages of its design.
2 Think about a public space in your city or town. Which aspects of its design do you like? What would you change about it in order to improve it?

ACADEMIC KEYWORDS

preserve (v) /prɪˈzɜrv/
convert (v) /kənˈvɜrt/
unique (adj) /juˈnik/

READING 2 Designing solutions

Before you read

What are some solutions humans have devised to overcome challenges in the following areas?

- Agriculture/Farming
- Housing
- Transportation

THINK ABOUT:

weather

water

limited space

environmental issues

energy efficiency

geographical challenges

Global reading

1 Scan *Designing solutions* and complete the chart about the two construction projects.

Name of project	Location	Year started	Reasons for project
1			
2			

RECOGNIZING CAUSE AND EFFECT

Written passages often describe a cause–effect relationship between two events. This relationship can be described using different patterns.

Poor road design often **results in** *traffic problems*. (cause → effect)

Traffic problems **are** often **the result of** *poor road design*. (effect → cause)

It is important to be able to recognize these patterns when you read, so that you can clearly understand these connections. Other verbs:

cause → effect	effect → cause
cause, bring about, lead to, result of, give rise to	*because of, be due to, be caused by, result from, thanks to*

2 Read *Designing solutions* again. Then match the causes 1–6 with the effects a–f.

Causes

1 concerns about population growth, climate change, and aging infrastructures _____

2 rapidly growing population, lack of farmland _____

3 developing the New Valley _____

4 the finished project _____

5 the shifting landscape (in Venice) _____

6 record high flood water _____

Effects

a city endures flooding 60 times a year

b relieve problems, such as overcrowding and food shortages

c Egyptian government began work on the New Valley

d some of the most daring engineering projects ever attempted

e destruction of historical landmarks and artistic masterpieces

f increase in Egypt's usable land by 25%

Close reading

What types of information do you need in order to answer these questions?
Scan *Designing solutions* to find the answers.

1 What are the three biggest challenges facing the world today?
2 How much did the Pumping Station cost to build?
3 How much water is it capable of pumping?
4 By what percentage might the project increase Egypt's usable land?
5 How much do experts say Venice has sunk in the past 100 years?
6 How big are the flood gates?

ACADEMIC KEYWORDS		
population	(n)	/ˌpɒpjəˈleɪʃ(ə)n/
transform	(v)	/trænsˈfɔrm/
complex	(adj)	/kəmˈpleks/

Designing solutions

[1] Since their earliest beginnings, humans have devised ways to improve their living conditions. Over time we have developed incredibly clever solutions to overcome challenges of limited space and extreme climates and geography, creating stronger, more efficient buildings, and faster, more convenient forms of transportation. Today's engineers and architects seem able to create the impossible — building higher, longer, more complex structures than ever before.

[2] Population growth, climate change, and aging urban infrastructures are some of the dilemmas affecting the world today. In some places, these concerns have brought about some of the biggest, most daring engineering projects ever attempted — projects that will redesign the course of nature.

1 New Valley Project, Egypt

[3] The New Valley Project is an ambitious plan to transform half a million acres of dry, barren desert into a man-made valley of fertile farmland. The Egyptian government began work on the New Valley Project in 1997 to deal with the problems it faced due to the country's rapidly growing population and lack of farmland. The hope is that developing the new valley will help relieve problems such as overcrowding and food shortages by providing land for agriculture as well as new living space for up to three million people.

[4] How will this be possible? The project involves transporting water from the River Nile to the Western Desert of Egypt (part of the Sahara Desert). The Pumping Station at the heart of the project, which cost $436 million to build, was completed in 2005. An amazing feat of engineering in itself, the station has 24 pumps with adjustable speed settings. When the entire project is completed, the station will pump over 1.2 million cubic meters of water per hour into a system of canals which will carry the water 360 kilometers to the valley. No one can say for certain whether the project will be successful in the long term. However, by 2020, when construction of the New Valley Project is scheduled for completion, supporters say the finished project will result in an increase in Egypt's usable land by as much as 25% and allow the country to completely meet its own food requirements. On the other hand, opponents say the project is too costly and allows Egypt to use too much of the Nile's precious water, which may have a negative effect on other countries that rely on the water too.

2 Venice Tide Barrier Project, Italy

[5] The Italian city of Venice is known as one of the most beautiful, romantic places in the world. Venice is famous for its rich cultural heritage, beautiful architecture, and Renaissance art — and famous for floods. Since written records about Venice's water levels began in 1872, floods have been a part of its history. The city is situated in a lagoon in the Adriatic Sea and experts say it has sunk as much as 23 centimeters in the last century. As a result of the shifting landscape, the city currently endures flooding about 60 times a year according to some estimates. Since 1966, when record high flood waters caused the destruction of numerous historical landmarks and artistic masterpieces, Venetians have been debating what to do. The Tide Barrier Project (also known as the MOSE project) was begun in 2003 by Silvio Berlusconi, who is Italy's former Prime Minister. It consists of 78 underwater steel gates, each around 28 meters high, 20 meters wide, and weighing 300 tons. The gates are attached to the sea floor. When a dangerously high tide is predicted, compressed air is pumped underneath the gates, causing them to rise and stop the sea water from overflowing into the city. Many people believe the project is the only way to save Venice. Others argue that it will have negative effects on wildlife, and simply won't stop the flooding.

[6] If successful, these projects have amazingly positive potential. They may be examples of today's 'where there's a will, there's a way' attitude. But is it really possible for humans to tame the sea or to turn the desert into a lush valley? Perhaps. Only time will tell.

Developing critical thinking

1 Discuss these questions in a group.

1 Describe how the design of the two projects in the article addressed a problem. Do you think they are effective solutions?

2 What effects do you think these projects will have on people's lives in the short term? In the long-term future?

2 Think about the ideas from *The Metropol Parasol* and *Designing solutions* and discuss these questions in a group.

1 What are some of the differing opinions about each project? Which opinions do you agree with?

2 Think of an area in your town, city, or country that could somehow be changed to improve residents' lives. Suggest ideas for redesigning and making improvements to the area. Discuss the pros and cons of each.

USEFUL LANGUAGE

Many people think ...

Opponents believe ...

Others argue that ...

Some people say that ...

THINK ABOUT:

community

green spaces

facilities

services

transport

modernization

Vocabulary skill

PREFIX *OVER-*

The prefix *over-* is used to add the meaning 'too much' to a word. For example, the word *overworked* describes someone who has worked too much. Consider these examples from the two reading texts:

*Opponents call it an **overpriced** eyesore. (overpriced = costing too much money)*

*The hope is that developing the New Valley will help relieve problems such as **overcrowding**. (overcrowding = a situation when a place has too many people)*

Complete the sentences with the correct form of the words in the box.

| confident | crowd | do | eat | estimate | flow | react | sleep |

1 This bath is poorly designed. It's not deep enough and sometimes it
_____.

2 That architect is a bit _____. He assumes his design is better than all the rest.

3 I can't work out how to set my new alarm clock correctly, so yesterday
I _____.

4 I think the designer _____. He didn't need to shout at me. I only said that we might need to change a few details.

5 The construction company _____ the cost of the project. It was much less expensive than they had expected.

6 We need to do something about the _____ in our cities. There are too many people and there's not enough housing.

7 I prefer simple designs. I think they've _____ the colors and patterns in this room.

8 Many people _____ and gain weight when they are under stress.

WRITING The pros and cons of a design

You are going to learn about using transitions for introducing opposing ideas and practice using non-defining relative clauses. You are then going to use these to write a description of a building or structure and discuss the pros and cons (positive and negative points) of its design.

Writing skill

TRANSITIONS: INTRODUCING OPPOSING IDEAS

To express contrasting opinions or ideas within one sentence

To do this effectively in your writing you can use the following words and phrases (or transitions) to signal the opposing idea: *although, despite, even though, however, in contrast to, in spite of, whereas,* and *while*.

Whereas *the new opera house is beautiful inside, the large dome on top does not seem to fit the building.*

While *the bridge will improve transportation problems downtown, the project will cost too much money.*

To express an opposing idea in a new sentence

We can express an opinion in one sentence, and then use the transition to express an opposing idea in the next sentence using the following expressions: *on the other hand, nevertheless, it can also be said that,* and *yet*.

The new opera house is beautiful inside. **However**, *the large dome on top does not seem to fit the building.*

The bridge will definitely improve transportation problems downtown. **On the other hand**, *the project will cost too much money.*

Use the transitions in parentheses to combine these opposing ideas. You may use one or two sentences.

1 The bridge is modern and attractive. / There are many safety concerns. (however)

2 The city needed a new hotel. / The building is ugly and won't help attract tourists. (although)

3 Many people like modern, futuristic design. / I prefer traditional architecture. (whereas)

4 The Sky Mall isn't conveniently located. / It has amazing views from the rooftop garden. (on the other hand)

5 The parking lot may help local businesses. / It will destroy a natural wildlife habitat. (nevertheless)

Grammar

NON-DEFINING RELATIVE CLAUSES

Non-defining relative clauses begin with the relative pronouns **who** or **which**. They are used to add extra information to a sentence.

Metropol Parasol was designed by Jürgen Mayer H., **who** *is a German architect*.

The Pumping Station, **which** *cost $436 million to build*, *was completed in 2005.*

When added to the end of the sentence, non-defining relative clauses require a comma before the relative pronoun. When the clause is placed in the middle of the sentence, use a comma both before and after it.

1 **Complete the sentences with the relative clauses in the box. Add commas where they are needed.**

which closed last year	which is a great place to eat lunch
which was incredibly romantic	which houses the mayor's office
who works for a design firm	who was a friend from my university days

1 City Hall _____ has a large golden dome on the top.

2 My cousin Casey _____ is one of my favorite relatives.

3 The new student center has a large outdoor area _____.

4 Last month I saw Jim Stafford _____.

5 We saw a lot of iconic buildings on our trip to India. We even got to watch the sunset over the Taj Mahal _____.

6 The old school on West Street _____ was built in 1792.

2 **Complete the sentences with your own information. Use a relative clause in each sentence.**

1 One famous landmark I have visited _____
_____.

2 A well-known designer from my country _____
_____.

3 One of the oldest buildings in my city _____
_____.

4 An example of traditional architecture from my country _____
_____.

5 Modern architectural design _____
_____.

6 Someday, I'd like to visit _____
_____.

WRITING TASK

Write about a building or structure which interests you.

Audience: classmates/peers
Context: a description of a location, building, or structure with regard to its design
Purpose: to evaluate and express opinions about the pros and cons of the design of a public space

BRAINSTORM

1 Read the text about an interesting building. Circle the transitions the writer used for adding opposing ideas. Underline the non-defining relative clauses.

The new Shankman Sports Complex, which was completed in March 2012, is a brand new sports facility. The complex is 3,000 meters squared. It has several floors and includes an Olympic-sized swimming pool, a hockey rink, basketball and volleyball courts, and a weight-training room with a wide range of modern exercise equipment. The exterior of the building is all brick with a traditional rectangular shape and design. The entrance includes some welcoming decorative features, such as a fountain and a statue of the founder, Tom Shankman, who was a minor-league baseball player.

While the new complex offers lots of state-of-the-art equipment inside, the exterior appears too traditional and rather uninteresting, in my opinion. If I were the architect, I would have added a few interestingly-shaped windows, a dome-roof, and I'd have used more modern-looking building materials. The complex has plenty of indoor space for athletics. However, there are no facilities for sports such as soccer or baseball, which are best played outdoors. Part of the problem is the location. City planners chose the site of the old Denby Elementary School. Although this is a convenient location, it did not allow outdoor facilities nor enough parking space.

Despite these minor design issues, the Shankman Sports Complex is certain to be a busy place year round.

2 Think of interesting buildings (or structures or engineering projects, such as a bridge, monument, or park) anywhere in the world.

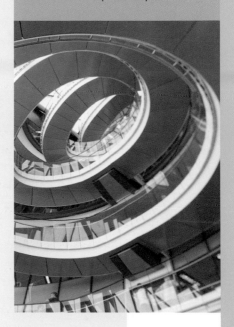

PLAN

Make some notes about what you like and dislike about one of the buildings or structures. Think about the following in relation to the design:

- Appearance
- Location
- Size
- Purpose and functionality
- Shape
- Any other features you have an opinion about

WRITE

Write two-paragraphs about the building or structure.

- In the first paragraph, describe the building or structure in detail.
- In the second paragraph, discuss the pros and cons of its design and suggest ideas for improving it.

Where possible, use transitions for introducing opposing ideas and non-defining relative clauses.

SHARE

1 Exchange papers with a partner. Read the checklist on page 109 and provide feedback to your partner. Also think about the following points:

- Do the paragraphs describe both the pros and cons of the design?
- Did the writer use transitions for opposing ideas?
- Did the writer correctly use non-defining relative clauses?
- Do you have any suggests to improve the paragraphs?

2 Discuss your writing and provide feedback to your partner.

REWRITE AND EDIT

Consider your partner's comments and rewrite your description.

STUDY SKILLS Editing and proofreading strategies

Getting started

Discuss these questions with a partner.

1 When do you edit or proofread your writing? Make a list of all of the different times you edit your writing, both in various courses and outside of school. When do you do your most careful editing? Why?

2 How do you edit or proofread your own writing?

3 Do you ever ask a classmate to check your writing? Why or why not?

Scenario

Read the scenario and think about what Ramon did right and what he did wrong.

Consider it

Read the tips about editing and proofreading strategies. Discuss each one with a partner. Which strategies do you already use? Which new strategies would be useful for you to try? Why?

1 **Edit for ideas and organization** Check that your writing is well-organized and that your main ideas are supported with details, examples, or reasons, depending on the type of writing you are doing. Check that each paragraph has a topic sentence and a concluding sentence.

2 **Do a reverse outline** Instead of writing an outline *before* your first draft, try doing an outline based on your *final* draft. By doing this, you can check that each of your main points in your paragraph or essay has enough support. You will see where you need to add more information.

3 **Create a personal editing checklist** Look at one or two of your corrected papers and see what your most common errors are and how to correct them. Then make a checklist, listing your most typical errors. Use categories, such as subject–verb agreement, word choice, singular and plural of nouns, capitalization, and so on. Then, when you edit, check for your most common problem. Just look for that type of error. Then check your writing again for your second most common error.

4 **Read backwards** Check for errors in grammar, punctuation, and capitalization by reading your paper from the end, going backwards sentence by sentence.

5 **Ask a classmate to read your paper** Even professional writers have an editor. This is because others can see errors and problems that we cannot. You don't need to follow every suggestion your classmate makes, but notice what is unclear to your classmate.

Over to you

Discuss these questions with a partner.

1 Why do you think it is important to become skilled at editing and proofreading?

2 What other strategies or resources could you use for editing your own writing?

3 What are the advantages and disadvantages of asking a classmate to check your written work?

At the beginning of the term, Ramon was struggling in his writing class. When he received his first papers back from the teacher, the teacher always noted that Ramon needed to edit his writing and proofread it for grammar, spelling, and punctuation. However, Ramon always checked his writing before he handed it in. He would read it over once or twice, making a few corrections to the spelling. After getting back several marked papers from the teacher, Ramon realized that he wasn't seeing all of his errors. Also, as the teacher pointed out, he had many different types of errors; errors in the overall organization of his ideas, errors in grammar, and errors in capitalization and punctuation, which Ramon considered to be very minor errors. There seemed to be so many errors that Ramon didn't know where to focus his attention when editing. He decided to meet with the teacher and find out how he could improve his editing.

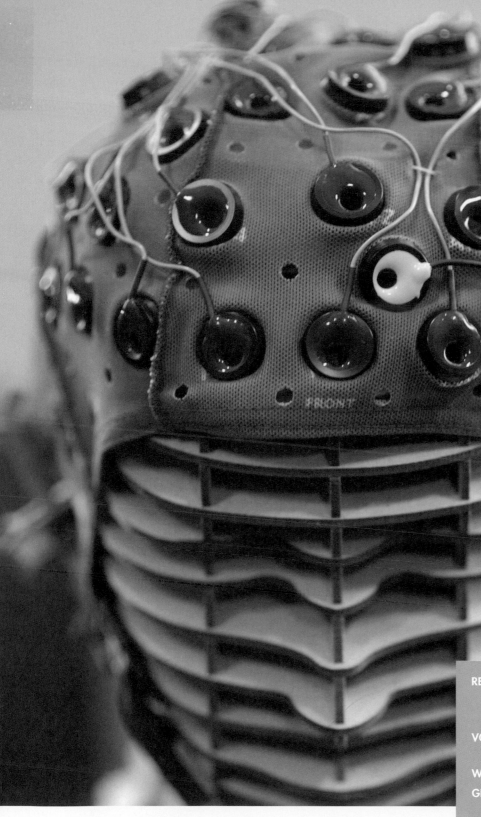

Thought

READING	Skimming
	Understanding vocabulary from context
VOCABULARY	Collocations: noun + verb
WRITING	Summarizing
GRAMMAR	Adverb clauses of reason and purpose

Discussion point

Discuss these questions with a partner.

1 When you are studying, what kinds of things help you to concentrate? What things distract you? Make two lists.

2 Do you think you have a good memory? What are you good (or poor) at remembering?

3 How does modern technology affect the way we learn and study?

Vocabulary preview

Complete the sentences with the words in the box.

accuracy	challenge	concentrate	efficiency	evidence	expand
performance	study				

1 _____ has shown that exercise has a positive effect on memory.

2 In our class, we discussed the results of a recent _____ on the eating habits of teenagers.

3 When you measure chemicals, _____ is very important.

4 After increasing his hours at the gym, his _____ in swim competitions greatly improved.

5 Good time management improves _____ in the workplace.

6 The ability to _____ for a long time is rare in young children.

7 Next year, the university plans to _____ the library.

8 My biggest _____ this year is to keep up with my assignments.

READING 1 Is your memory online?

Before you read

Discuss these questions with a partner.

1 What do you use the Internet for?

2 Do you think that the Internet makes students today better (or less) informed than students 50 years ago? Why?

3 How do you know the information you find on the Internet is accurate?

THINK ABOUT:
academic research
finding information
news
weather

Global reading

SKIMMING

Skimming (reading an article very quickly to get the main idea) is useful for reading a lot of material or for reading an article very quickly to see if you should read it more carefully.

Here are steps and tips for skimming:

1 Read the title, any subtitles, and captions of photographs.

2 Read the first paragraph.

3 Read only the first and last sentence of every paragraph.

4 Read the last paragraph completely.

1 **Skim *Is your memory online?* in one minute. Follow the steps and tips in the skill box.**

2 **Without looking back at *Is your memory online?*, circle the best word in the sentences.**

1 The article is about memory and **books / the Internet**.

2 It discusses finding **photos / information** on the Internet.

3 It discusses some **experiments / tests**.

4 People's memories are becoming **worse / different** because of the Internet.

5 This article has information about **research / universities**.

ACADEMIC KEYWORDS

conduct	(v)	/kənˈdʌkt/
dependent	(adj)	/dɪˈpendənt/
specific	(adj)	/spəˈsɪfɪk/

Is your memory online?

[1] If you are trying to find out who invented algebra or what language they speak on the island of Aruba, do you ask a friend, go to the library, or look it up online? These days, most people will look it up online with a quick Internet search. 'Just Google it', people say, using the name of the popular Internet search engine. As Internet users become more dependent on the Internet to store information, are people remembering less? If you know your computer will save information, why store it in your own personal memory, your brain? Experts are wondering if the Internet is changing what we remember and how.

[2] In a recent study, psychologist Betsy Sparrow of Columbia University in New York conducted four different experiments. She and her research team wanted to know how the Internet is changing memory. In the first experiment, they gave people 40 unimportant facts to type into a computer. The first group of people understood that the computer would save the information. The second group understood that the computer would not save it. Later, the second group remembered the information better. People in the first group knew they could find the information again, so they did not try to remember it.

[3] In another experiment, the researchers gave people facts to remember. In addition, the researchers told them where to find the information on the computer. The information was in a specific computer folder. Surprisingly, people later remembered the folder location better than the facts. When people use the Internet, they do not remember the information. Rather, they remember how to find it.

[4] This is called 'transactive memory'. In transactive memory, we remember where to find the information, but we don't remember the information. Before the Internet, people used transactive memory to remember which person or book had the information they needed. Now, instead of asking a friend or classmate for information, people use the Internet. With the Internet, endless information is available. We don't have to remember the information, but we do have to remember where it is stored.

[5] According to Sparrow, we are not becoming people with poor memories as a result of the Internet. Instead, computer users are developing stronger transactive memories; that is, people are learning how to organize huge quantities of information so that they are able to access it at a later date. This doesn't mean we are becoming either more or less intelligent, but there is no doubt that the way we use memory is changing.

Close reading

Read a student's notes about *Is your memory online?* Find eight errors and correct them.

Notes on 'Is Your Memory Online?'
1 *Psychologist at Columbia University conducted 3 experiments*
  Aim: How is the Internet changing students?
2 *Experiment: people typed words into a computer*
  1st group: knew computer wouldn't save information   2nd group: knew computer would save information
  Result: 1st group remembered the info better
3 *Experiment: gave people info to remember and where to find the folder with the information on the computer*
  Result: Later, people remembered the location of the info better than the name of the folder
4 *Transactive memory: we forget where to find the information we need*
5 *Conclusion: because of the Internet, our transactive memory is becoming weaker*

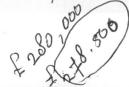

Developing critical thinking

Discuss these questions in a group.

1 What kinds of information do you think it is good to let the Internet 'remember' for you? What kinds of information do you need to remember?

2 Do you think that you remember the location of information (where to find it) better than the actual information? Why or why not?

READING 2 How does the brain multitask?

Before you read

Think of three examples of multitasking from your daily life. Which situation is the easiest for you, and why?

Global reading

1 **Skim *How does the brain multitask?* in one minute. Write *T* (True) or *F* (False).**

  1 The topic of this reading is the Internet. ___
  2 The article gives information about current research on multitasking. ___
  3 The article gives information about how to improve your study skills. ___
  4 The main idea of the reading is that when you multitask, you make more mistakes. ___

2 **Answer the questions.**

  1 What kinds of technology make it easy for individuals to multitask?
  2 Why did the researchers use MRIs in the experiment?

Close reading

1 **Read *How does the brain multitask?* again and answer the questions.**

  1 What was the difference between the two groups in paragraph 3?
  2 What was the result of that experiment?
  3 How did the researchers find this out?
  4 According to the experiments, how does multitasking affect your work?
  5 Why is it sometimes possible to multitask efficiently while cooking or washing dishes?

UNDERSTANDING VOCABULARY FROM CONTEXT

To read effectively, it is important to keep reading even when you meet a word you don't know. Don't stop to look up words the first time you read an article but try to guess new words by looking at the context. When you read an article a second time, look up important words if you are still unsure of the meaning.

2 **Find these words in *How does the brain multitask?* Read the sentences before and after the word. Then decide what the word means, using only the context.**

  1 high-tech (paragraph 1)
  2 electronic media (paragraph 1)
  3 prefrontal cortex (paragraphs 2 and 3)
  4 simultaneously (paragraph 3)
  5 switching (paragraph 3)
  6 declines (paragraph 4)
  7 limit (paragraph 5)
  8 lyrics (paragraph 6)

How does the
BRAIN MULTITASK?

[1] In a university library, a student is writing an essay on his laptop. But that's not all. He's also reading instant messages online, listening to his music with headphones, and checking text messages on his cell phone. He is the picture of high-tech multitasking. In today's world, people use a wide variety of electronic media to multitask, doing several things at the same time. Neuroscientists are studying the brain to see what happens during multitasking and to see if multitasking affects the quality of what we do.

[2] Using Magnetic Resonance Imaging (MRI) to view the brain in action, scientists have found that when people do tasks that require concentration, multitasking takes place in the prefrontal cortex. Data shows that the prefrontal cortex, located in the front of the brain, is the area for problem solving, decision making, planning, and emotions.

[3] In a multitasking study conducted by French scientists Etienne Koechlin and Sylvain Charron, people were given one task requiring concentration (sorting letters and shapes). Brain images showed that both the left and right prefrontal cortex were active as people worked. However, when they gave a person a second task to do at the same time, the left prefrontal cortex took one task, and the right took the other. When doing two tasks, MRI images showed that the brain was rapidly switching between the first and the second task. The brain was not working on both tasks at the same time. These experiments, and others like them, show that the brain is not paying attention to two tasks simultaneously. When multitasking, the brain is concentrating on one task and then switching to the other, in sequence.

[4] In order to switch attention from one task to another, the brain must use its working memory. This is the brain's ability to temporarily hold information while it does something else. When you multitask, you 'leave' a task that is not finished. It is as if you are reading a book and your brain puts in a bookmark when you leave the task. The first task is stored in your working memory. Your brain goes to the second task, but when it returns to the first task, it must restart the task, using working memory. Because working memory declines with age, older people do not multitask as well as teenagers and young adults. Young children also do not multitask well because their working memory is not fully developed.

[5] Although we think we are getting more done when we multitask, evidence shows that we do not. Researchers have found that people take longer to complete tasks and make more mistakes. Furthermore, doing more tasks seems to result in less efficiency. When the French researchers expanded their experiment to include three tasks, surprisingly, the brain seemed to completely drop one task and only focus on two tasks. The French team concluded that the brain could not focus on more than two tasks at a time. Perhaps there is a limit to how much information the brain can temporarily store in working memory.

[6] More experiments are needed to see how multitasking works in different real-life situations. Students multitask as they study, office workers constantly check e-mail while they work, and drivers talk on the phone or text. Of course, certain tasks such as listening to music do not require as much concentration as others. Data shows that studying while listening to music without lyrics usually does not affect performance. Some daily tasks such as driving, cooking, or washing dishes, become almost automatic with practice, requiring less concentration. However, when a driver is multitasking, the seconds lost when mentally switching tasks can result in an accident.

[7] Researchers have shown that when we multitask, we are not really getting more done because we are losing speed and accuracy as we quickly switch from task to task. Experts say that for a task that requires your concentration, it's better to just focus on that one task until you are done. The challenge in today's world of 24/7 connection to electronic media is how to control our desire to do many things at once.

ACADEMIC KEYWORDS

concentration	(n)	/ˌkɑnsənˈtreɪʃ(ə)n/
decline	(v)	/dɪˈklaɪn/
evidence	(n)	/ˈevɪdəns/

Developing critical thinking

1 Discuss these questions in a group.

1   Do you think that you are less accurate when you are multitasking? Why or why not?

2   When do you think it is a bad idea to multitask? Explain your answer.

2 Think about the ideas from *Is your memory online?* and *How does the brain multitask?* and discuss these questions in a group.

1   Both readings are based on research results. Which research seems more reliable? Why?

2   In education, should teachers encourage students to use transactive memory and multitasking? Why or why not?

Vocabulary skill

COLLOCATIONS: NOUN + VERB

A collocation is a pair of words that are commonly found together. When you learn a word, make a note of the words that are usually found with it. Look at these verbs that are commonly found in academic English and the nouns they frequently collocate with:

adopt + *position, attitude, style, process, measure, method, approach, lifestyle, policy, child*

address + *problem, issue, topic, question, audience, class, person, letter*

analyze + *facts, data, information, evidence, results, samples*

conduct + *audit, experiment, inquiry, inspection, interview, investigation, research, review, search, study, survey, test*

1 Complete the sentences with the correct form of a verb from the skill box. More than one answer may be possible.

1   The students _____ some research into memory and _____ the results.

2   Last week the police _____ a full inquiry into the accident and _____ the evidence.

3   The head teacher _____ a serious tone when he _____ the question of cheating.

4   When the chemists _____ the research findings, they discovered that the initial experiment had not been _____ under controlled conditions.

5   For our final exam, we will have to _____ the lab results from two different studies.

6   Let's _____ the real problem here. I think you are _____ an unnecessarily aggressive attitude.

2 Complete the sentences using a noun from the skill box.

1   There was a newspaper article in yesterday's paper which analyzed _____

2   In the chemistry lab, students conducted _____

3   Yesterday, my manager conducted _____

4   In my research paper, I aim to analyze _____

5   In order to find out students' opinions about this issue, we will conduct ____

6   The government has adopted _____

7   Next Wednesday, the history professor will address _____

WRITING A summary and a response paragraph

You are going to learn about summarizing and using adverb clauses of reason and purpose. You are then going to use these to write a summary paragraph and a response paragraph.

Writing skill

SUMMARIZING

When you summarize, you give the main ideas of a reading in your own words. A summary can be short (one sentence) or it can be several sentences. Depending on the length, you may include a few supporting points, but you should not include details.

Summarizing is a skill you need for writing a response to a text. In addition, summarizing after you read is a good way to check your reading comprehension.

Here are some questions to help you summarize:

*   What is the reading about (the topic)?
*   What are some of the key words and phrases? (List at least four.)
*   What does the author say about the topic?

1 Skim *Is your memory online?* to review the article. Complete the summary.

In the article '(1) _____,' the author discusses research about Internet users and (2) _____. There were several (3) _____ to see if Internet users use their memory differently. Researchers found that Internet users (4) _____ where to find information better than what the information is. The author says that people are developing strong transactive (5) _____, but it is not clear if people have weaker memories.

2 Answer questions about the summary in exercise 1.

  1 Which sentence gives the topic of the text? What is the topic?
  2 What are four key words or phrases in the summary?
  3 What conclusion did the researchers reach?
  4 Write one sentence to summarize the text.

3 Write a short paragraph summarizing *How does the brain multitask?* To guide your writing, think about the questions in the skill box. Use the summary in exercise 1 as a model.

Grammar

ADVERB CLAUSES OF REASON AND PURPOSE

To introduce or explain a reason or purpose, we can use an adverb clause. An adverb clause is a dependent clause which can come either at the beginning of a sentence, followed by a comma, or at the end. (See page 14.)

Since the brain cannot focus on more than one task at a time, *it has to put one task on hold while it deals with another.*

As I have a smart phone, *I can easily check my email messages.*

*People are learning how to organize huge quantities of information **so that they are able to access it at a later date***

Reason: *because, since, as, due to the fact that*

Purpose: *so that, in order to*

1 **Complete the sentences with an adverb clause of reason or purpose. More than one answer may be possible.**

  1 Could you give me your data _____ I can analyze it tonight?

  2 _____ I needed to concentrate on my homework, I turned off my cell phone.

  3 My uncle often switches back and forth between English and Arabic _____ he is bilingual.

  4 We had to wait at the restaurant for an hour _____ we didn't have a reservation.

  5 A survey is being conducted _____ find out which activities are the most popular with students.

2 **Answer the questions, giving a reason or a purpose. Write complete sentences, including an adverb clause and an independent clause.**

  1 Why are you studying English?

  2 Why do you use the Internet?

  3 What do you sometimes do to focus on your studies?

  4 What happens when you try to do too many things at once? Give an example.

  5 When and where do you have your best ideas? Explain.

WRITING TASK

Write a summary and response to a blog posting about multitasking.

Audience:	teacher and students
Context:	academic
Purpose:	to respond to a reading assignment

BRAINSTORM

1 Read the response paragraph to a blog posting about giving up multitasking for a week. What was the student's experience? Underline one adverb clause of reason and one of purpose.

Discussion board

Ungraded question, posted by Professor T. Sperling

This week's lecture covered how the brain multitasks. In next week's class we're going to be considering multitasking further, with specific reference to the impact it has on stress levels. Before the class post your ideas on the impact (either positive or negative) that performing several tasks at once has on your life.

In order to examine how multitasking may cause stress in my own life, I decided to try the author's no-multitasking experiment. However, I only eliminated multitasking for one day. Like the author, I felt much calmer when I just focused on one task. I noticed that my concentration was much better and that I seemed to be more creative in solving problems. However, unlike the author, I found it very hard to break the habit of multitasking. When my cell phone rang, it interrupted my thoughts, even if I didn't answer the call. I learned that multitasking is a very strong habit for me. It would be interesting to set up a school experiment so that we could learn how other students experience a few days of no multitasking.

2 Re-read *Is your memory online?* or *How does the brain multitask?* As you read, write notes in the margin. Note if you agree or disagree with the text, what your opinion is, and what your personal experience is. This will prepare you for writing a response.

PLAN

Make a rough outline of your response paragraph. Include the following information:

1 What ideas in the article do you agree with? Why? Can you give examples from your own life?
2 What ideas in the article do you disagree with? Why? Can you give examples?
3 Do you think this is an important area for more research? Why or why not?

WRITE

Using either the model from *Is your memory online?* (exercise 1, page 33) or what you wrote about *How does the brain multitask?* (exercise 3, page 33) as the basis, write a fuller summary, adding at least two sentences to this paragraph. Then write your response paragraph.

SHARE

Exchange paragraphs with a partner. Read the checklist on page 109 and provide feedback to your partner.

REWRITE AND EDIT

Consider your partner's comments and write a final draft.

Plagiarism

by Stella Cottrell

What is plagiarism?

Plagiarism is using the work of others without acknowledging your source of information or inspiration. This includes:

- using words more or less exactly as they have been used in articles, lectures, television programs, books, or anywhere else
- using other people's ideas or theories without saying whose ideas they are
- paraphrasing (writing in other words) what you read or hear without stating where it comes from.

Even if you change words or sentences you have 'borrowed' or put them in a different order, the result is still plagiarism.

Plagiarism is treated very seriously, and plagiarized work is usually disqualified.

Using quotations

Quotations should be:

- used sparingly — and only if the words really are worth quoting
- brief — a few words or, at most, a few lines.

In writing a quotation you should:

- copy words and punctuation exactly
- use three dots (…) to indicate omitted words
- put 'quotation marks' around the words you quote (e.g. '*Stunning,*' *wrote the artist.*)
- say exactly where the quotation comes from.

Develop confidence in your own words

Use your own words, even if you don't think you write well — they count for more than copied text.

How to avoid plagiarism

- Write all your notes in your own words.
- Note down exactly where you read the information you put in your notes.
- In your assignment, write out where ideas and information come from:
  - reference your work
  - make it clear when you are using a direct quotation
  - write a full list of references and, if required, a bibliography (all the books and other materials you used).

If you have a habit of copying:

- Put your pen out of reach.
- Read a passage without taking any notes.
- Stop reading and cover up the page.
- Sum up what you have read. If possible, talk aloud, or record yourself, so you hear your own words and in your own voice.
- Once you can say what the passage is about, note it down in your own words.
- If you want to copy material to use as a quotation, write it in a different color so that you can find it easily. The color will also show you how much you copy.

Other people's words make a poor lifeboat

Fire

READING	Summarizing
	Identifying steps in a sequence
VOCABULARY	American and British English: *have to* vs. *have got to*
WRITING	Using sensory details in a narrative
GRAMMAR	Adverbs as stance markers

Discussion point

1 **Match the expressions below to their meanings. Do you have any sayings about fire in your first language? What are they? Explain their meanings.**

1 to play with fire ___

2 to jump out of the frying pan and into the fire ___

3 Where there's smoke, there's fire. ___

4 to come under fire ___

a If something bad is being said about someone or something, it is probably partly true.

b to become involved in a dangerous situation

c to be criticized

d to go from one bad situation to a worse one

2 **Think of a story, situation, or experience that can be described by one of the expressions above. Use the expression to explain it to a partner.**

Vocabulary preview

Read the sentences. Circle the correct meaning of the words in bold.

1 Jobs in technology are very **competitive**. You need a lot of work experience.
   a attracting a lot of people   b easy to find

2 Water is a **compound** of hydrogen and oxygen.
   a the opposite   b mixture

3 Most children enjoy watching fireworks, but my son is an **exception**.
   a someone who is large   b someone who is different

4 When mountain climbing, make sure you bring **gear** for cold weather.
   a equipment   b food

5 The police are interviewing students about an **incident** at the school.
   Someone pulled the fire alarm as a joke.
   a event   b place

6 Thankfully, the doctor said that Tom's burns were not **life-threatening**.
   a likely to cause death   b likely to heal quickly

7 Please read the safety manual and follow the **procedures** carefully.
   a steps   b amount of time

8 You should keep all explosive **substances** away from heat.
   a materials   b children

READING 1 Feeling the heat

Before you read

What different duties do firefighters usually perform? What kinds of dangers do they face? Discuss with a partner.

Global reading

> ### SUMMARIZING
>
> A summary should give only the key information from the original text.
> It should *not* use exact sentences from the text, or include a lot of details.
> Use your own words and give only the important points. Do not add extra
> information that isn't in the text or express your own opinion. The information
> in the summary may not be in the same order as in the original text.

1 **Read *Feeling the heat*, an interview with a British firefighter. Write one sentence to summarize each paragraph.**

2 **Re-read the second paragraph, the answer to the question, *How would you describe what you do?* and choose the best summary below.**

a A firefighter can be called on to put out small rubbish fires, large brush or forest fires. They also respond to emergency medical calls like car accidents. When they aren't fighting fires, they visit businesses like restaurants and construction sites to educate people about fire safety and prevention. Most fires could have been prevented if people were better prepared.

b Firefighters have a variety of different duties. They have to fight all kinds of fires and respond to medical emergencies. They also work in the community teaching people how to prevent fires.

c Being a firefighter is a really interesting job. They put out small and large fires and help injured people. My uncle works as a firefighter, and he says the schedule and the pay are great. Firefighters also go into the community and help people learn how to stop fires before they start. I'm thinking about becoming a firefighter after I graduate.

FEELING THE HEAT: An interview with a British firefighter

[1] When faced with a life-threatening situation, like being inside a burning building, human instinct is to run away to avoid being hurt or killed. There are, however, exceptions to every rule. We recently spoke with a man whose job is to run towards danger, straight into buildings filled with flames, smoke, and explosive substances. Kevin Lynch is a firefighter with the London Fire Brigade. Read our interview to find out what it takes to become a professional firefighter and learn the ins and outs of this extremely dangerous but highly rewarding career.

[2] **Q: How would do describe what you do?**

A: A firefighter can be called on to do anything from putting out small rubbish fires to fighting a large fire in a factory or warehouse — anytime there's an incident involving fire. We also respond to medical emergency calls, like car accidents. When we aren't actively fighting fires, we work in the community, visiting schools, construction sites, and businesses to educate people about fire safety and prevention. It's a fact that most fires could have been prevented if people were better prepared and knew more about fire safety. We've got to try to stop fires before they even start.

[3] **Q: What kinds of training or skills are required for the job?**

A: It's an extremely competitive field, and difficult to get into. There's no upper age limit but you've got to be in excellent physical condition. For most fire brigades, it's a three-stage process. You've got to pass a challenging written exam, as well as an oral interview and a series of physical tests. And, of course, we've got to understand the science of fire, how it reacts with different chemical compounds, and how it behaves. For example, at a fire scene, we've got to assess the situation quickly and make split-second decisions about which doors and windows to open to let smoke out and oxygen in, without making the fire more serious. In that sense, I suppose another important skill is the ability to stay calm when things seem like they are falling apart.

[4] **Q: Do you ever feel afraid?**

A: Yeah, of course. Sometimes, we're out there risking our lives. Naturally, I feel some fear from time to time, but I can't think of a more rewarding job. A few months ago, we were called to a fire in a block of flats. It was quite a serious situation. One man had got badly burnt, then jumped out of the window and seriously injured himself when he landed on the pavement. Another man was trapped in the lift. Honestly, I've got to admit that I was nervous. On the way there, we heard on the radio that there were still two young lads in a flat on the second floor. Well, that made me get over my fear quickly. Unfortunately, a lot of children are afraid when they see us firefighters in all our gear. They don't understand that we're there to help them, and they run away or hide. Fortunately, in this case the kids didn't do that. We went straight up to the second floor, grabbed them, and got them outside to safety. The look on their mum's face was priceless. Amazingly, everyone in the building got out safely. At the end of the day, that's what it's all about for me — saving lives.

Close reading

Read *Feeling the heat* again and circle the answers.

1 Firefighters deal with **a range of situations / only situations involving fire**.
2 The process of becoming a firefighter includes **an interview and two tests / a written test and an oral interview**.
3 Firefighters need to be able to **make decisions quickly / keep everyone calm**.
4 According to Kevin Lynch, many children **are afraid when they see firefighters / want to become firefighters**.
5 Lynch states that he **doesn't think fear is natural / sometimes feels afraid**.

ACADEMIC KEYWORDS		
assess	(v)	/əˈses/
avoid	(v)	/əˈvɔɪd/
exception	(n)	ɪkˈsepʃ(ə)n/

Developing critical thinking

Discuss these questions in a group.

1 What are some other dangerous jobs/types of jobs that require people to risk their lives? Why do you think some people choose dangerous jobs?

2 Kevin Lynch says that an important skill for firefighters is to be able to 'stay calm when things are falling apart.' Do you have this skill? Give examples to explain why or why not. If you don't have this skill, do you know someone else who does?

READING 2 Fire in the sky

Before you read

Work with a partner. On what occasions are fireworks used in your culture? When do you see firework displays? Where do you go to watch them?

Global reading

Read *Fire in the sky*. Complete the summary of the history of fireworks.

Fireworks, also called pyrotechnics, have been used as a form of entertainment for centuries. The first firecrackers were made _____.

Later, between 600–900 CE, _____

_____.

In 1292, _____

During the Renaissance, _____

_____

By the 1700s in England _____

Today, _____

_____

Close reading

IDENTIFYING STEPS IN A SEQUENCE

Chronological organization (the order in which events happened) is a common pattern for historical texts, biographies, scientific texts, and others texts that explain detailed steps in a process. Learning to sequence ideas or steps from a text can help you understand the text correctly.

ACADEMIC KEYWORDS		
expand	(v)	/ɪkˈspænd/
primarily	(adv)	/praɪm(ə)rəli/
series	(n)	/ˈsɪriz/

Read the article again. Number these steps in the correct order.

___ **a** The Italians began to create fireworks for entertainment purposes.

___ **b** Chemists in China tried putting explosives into different types of containers.

___ **c** The English began having large firework displays that were open to the public.

___ **d** Fireworks from Asia were introduced to Italy by the explorer, Marco Polo.

___ **e** Wealthy Europeans started having fireworks displays at private celebrations.

___ **f** The Chinese began using bamboo 'firecrackers.'

FIRE   SKY

THE STORY OF PYROTECHNICS

[1] Pyrotechnics — or fireworks — have been lighting up the sky for centuries. The word *pyrotechnic* comes from the Greek words *pyro*, meaning fire, or burn, and *technic*, meaning art or skill. Today, these masterpieces of 'fire art' are used in celebrations and for entertainment all around the world. Read on to learn about the history of pyrotechnics and the science behind how they are made and how they work.

The earliest firecrackers

[2] A form of firecracker was used in China thousands of years ago even before gunpowder was invented. Historians believe that the tradition began around 200 BCE when someone threw a piece of green bamboo on the fire, when the dry wood ran out. Bamboo grows very quickly, creating pockets of air and sap in the stem, which expand and burst when heated. On the fire, it heated up, turned black, and finally exploded, causing a loud 'boom' and frightening everyone nearby. When people learned what had caused the noise, they began to find many uses for green bamboo. Farmers began to use it to scare wild animals away from their fields, and later, people began burning bamboo at parties, celebrations, and special occasions like weddings.

The invention of gunpowder

[3] Around 600–900 CE, Chinese chemists began to experiment, combining chemical substances to make louder, more powerful explosions. When they put these compounds inside a bamboo tube and lit them on fire, the firecracker was born. Eventually, they tried putting the chemicals into different types of containers. They knew that using a closed tube would blow up with a loud noise, but when placed in a container with an open end, the powder created bright flames, sparks, and thick smoke. These early fireworks were used primarily in warfare, to scare off enemies.

Fire art

[4] Somewhat later in 1292, the Italian explorer, Marco Polo, introduced Chinese fireworks to his home country. It was during the Renaissance (1400–1500) that the Italians began to explore the true art of pyrotechnics. The Italians modified military rockets by adding powdered metals and charcoal, which shot sprays of gold and silver sparks into the sky. They also built massive standing structures with torches, and fountains that gave off dramatic showers of sparks. Word spread quickly to other countries, and before long, fireworks displays were a common form of entertainment at celebrations of royalty and wealthy nobles around Europe. By the early 1700s in England, fireworks displays were often huge events open to the general public.

The choreography

[5] So, how do pyrotechnicians, today's fire artists, pull off these incredible feats of chemistry without incident? These days, while smaller shows may be fired with a series of electrical wires and switches, most larger fireworks displays are run by computer programs. Highly-trained professionals design the show and set up the fireworks in the correct order and placement. For these shows, technicians may set off between 40 and 50 thousand fireworks all within 30 minutes. According to one expert, it takes two hours of planning for every minute of firework choreography.

Developing critical thinking

1 Discuss these questions in a group.

1 Why do you think fireworks are such a popular form of entertainment at celebrations around the world? What do you think they symbolize?

2 What are some other ways fire is used for holidays and celebrations in your culture? What about in other cultures you know about?

2 Think about the ideas from *Feeling the heat* and *Fire in the sky* and discuss these questions in a group.

1 *Feeling the heat* stresses how fire can be dangerous and frightening, but *Fire in the sky* reminds us how people are attracted to it. Why do you think some people are attracted to danger in their lives?

2 Think about the other 'classical elements': air, water, and earth. In what ways can they be dangerous as well as life-giving?

Vocabulary skill

> **AMERICAN AND BRITISH ENGLISH: *HAVE TO* VS. *HAVE GOT TO***
>
> In American English, *have to (do something)* is used to express obligation:
> Firefighters often **have to** work long hours at the fire station.
> British English uses the phrase *have got to* in the same way:
> The fire destroyed John's house. He **has got to** rebuild the whole place.
> Note: In British English, the contracted forms are common with *have got to*: *I've got to, You've got to, He's/She's/It's got to, We've got to, They've got to.*

1 Work in pairs. Find and <u>underline</u> all of the examples of *have got to* in *Feeling the heat.*

2 Complete the sentences with the British English expression. Use the contracted form.

1 I'm afraid I can't come to tomorrow's meeting. I _____ work in the evening.

2 Karen nearly started a fire in the kitchen. She _____ be more careful.

3 There's no more wood for the campfire. We _____ get some before it gets dark.

4 Look! There are still people inside that burning building. They _____ get out quickly!

5 You _____ be careful with small children around. Don't leave matches or lighters in reach.

3 Work in pairs. Take turns completing the statements about obligations. Use *have got to*. Then say the statements again in American English.

1 This weekend, I _____.

2 Every day, my teacher _____.

3 A friend of mine _____.

4 As students in this class, we _____.

5 Firefighters in my country _____.

WRITING Narrative essay: A time when you faced danger

You are going to learn about using sensory details in a narrative and about using adverbs as stance markers. You are then going to use these to write a narrative essay about a time when you faced danger and describe your feelings and reactions in detail.

Writing skill

USING SENSORY DETAILS IN A NARRATIVE

When you describe an event or a personal experience in writing, it is helpful to use sensory details to 'paint a picture' for the reader. Sensory details describe events in terms of how they affect our five senses: sight, hearing, smell, taste, and touch. For example:

<u>Sight</u>: red-hot flames, smoke rising, blinding sunlight, the dark night

<u>Hearing</u>: a crackling fire, breaking glass, a heartbeat, a car's tires squealing

<u>Smell</u>: wood smoke, food cooking, fresh coffee

<u>Taste</u>: bitter medicine, sour, sweet, strong

<u>Touch</u>: summer heat, cool water, dry mouth, sharp pain

Using these types of descriptions can make your writing richer and more interesting to read.

Read a student's story about her hiking experience. Complete the text with the sensory details in the box.

bright, sunny	birds singing	colorful	fresh, clean-smelling
pinkish orange	rough and rocky	sharp pain	snap	steep, narrow

One [1]_____ summer afternoon, I went for a hike on Mount Morrison, a small mountain near my home with great hiking trails. I enjoyed the afternoon hiking in the [2]_____ mountain air, listening to the [3]_____, and taking pictures of the [4]_____ wildflowers. I reached the top of the mountain and the sky was turning [5]_____. Perfect, it was sunset. I had just enough time to get down the mountain before it got dark. On my way down, I saw a shortcut, a [6]_____ path down the side of the mountain. I had used it before, and it was much faster than the main trail, so I took it again. Sadly, it was the wrong choice. The path was [7]_____. It was starting to get dark, and I couldn't see well. My foot landed between two large rocks. As I fell, I heard a [8]_____ and felt a [9]_____. I had broken my ankle. Truthfully, I think it was the worst pain I had ever felt.

Grammar

ADVERBS AS STANCE MARKERS

Stance markers are words or phrases that express the writer's/speaker's feeling or attitude about something, for example, when describing a personal experience. Certain adverbs, usually placed at the beginning of a sentence, can be very useful for adding descriptive details and feeling to a piece of writing.

Surprisingly, many people don't have working smoke alarms in their homes.

When I finally met the firefighter who saved my life, I **honestly** couldn't speak.

There was a fire in the restaurant kitchen. **Luckily**, the chef was able to put it out quickly.

1 Choose the correct adverbs to complete this excerpt from *Feeling the heat*. Then check your answers on page 39.

Q: Do you ever feel afraid?
A: Yeah, of course. Sometimes, we're out there risking our lives. (1) **Naturally / Amazingly**, I feel some fear from time to time, but I can't think of a more rewarding job. A few months ago, we were called to a fire in a block of flats. It was quite a serious situation. … (2) **Amazingly / Honestly**, I've got to admit that I was nervous. On the way there, we heard on the radio that there were still two young lads in a flat on the second floor. Well, that made me get over my fear quickly. (3) **Unfortunately / Thankfully**, a lot of children are afraid when they see us firefighters in all our gear. They don't understand that we're there to help them, and they run away or hide. (4) **Fortunately / Sadly**, in this case, the kids didn't do that. We went straight up to the second floor, grabbed them, and got them outside to safety. The look on their mum's face was priceless. (5) **Naturally / Amazingly**, everyone in the building got out safely. That's what it's all about for me — saving lives.

2 Complete the student's narrative with the adverb stance markers in the box. More than one answer is possible.

amazingly   fortunately   happily   honestly   luckily   naturally
obviously   sadly   shockingly   surprisingly   thankfully   unfortunately

I was alone and injured, and it was getting dark fast. [1] _____, *my first thought was to call someone for help. Then I remembered I hadn't brought my cell phone! I called out, 'Help! Help!', but I couldn't hear anyone or anything.* [2] _____, *I didn't panic; somehow, I stayed calm and I felt confident that I would be OK.*

Then, about ten minutes later, I heard quick, loud footsteps running toward me. My heart was pounding. I closed my eyes. When I opened them, there was a large dog standing in front of me. He started to bark. Then I heard his owner call his name, 'Jackson!' [3] _____, *instead of running away, Jackson just stayed with me and kept barking until his owner followed the noise straight to us.*

[4] _____, *Jackson's owner, Stacey,* did *have a cell phone and was able to call for help. We're still friends today, and we often go hiking on Mount Morrison together.* [5] _____, *now I always remember my cell phone.*

WRITING TASK

Write about an experience when you faced a dangerous situation.

Audience: classmates/peers
Context: a personal narrative describing a dangerous or frightening experience
Purpose: to use sensory details and add emotion to a description

BRAINSTORM

Think of an experience when you faced danger. What was the situation? When was It? Where were you? Who were you with?

When

Where

Situation/Event

Who with

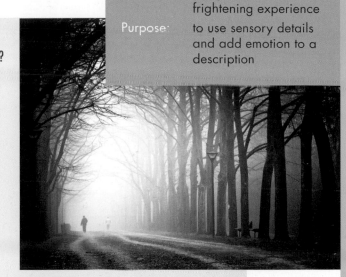

PLAN

Complete the chart with notes about the experience.

What happened (sequence of events)	How I felt	What I learned
1		
2		
3		
4		
5		
6		
7		
8		

WRITE

Write an essay about your experience. Describe the sequence of events in detail, including your feelings and what you learned from it. Where possible, use adverbs as stance markers and sensory details.

SHARE

Exchange papers with a partner. Read the checklist on page 109 and provide feedback to your partner. You can also think about these questions.

- Is the story easy to understand?
- Did the writer use sensory details to describe the events and make the story more interesting or exciting?
- Did the writer use adverbs as stance markers to indicate his or her attitude or feeling?
- What suggestions do you have to improve the story?
- What questions do you have about the story?

REWRITE AND EDIT

Consider your partner's comments and rewrite your narrative.

Managing stress

by Stella Cottrell

Stay relaxed

Sleep properly

- Aim to sleep for seven hours each day. More or less than this can make you feel tired.

Take breaks

- Give yourself regular breaks.

Use the STOP! exercise

- Let yourself stop everything for a moment. Breathe slowly or count to 100.
- Repeat 'stop' to yourself until you feel calm.

Monitor your state of mind

One aspect of stress is the attitude we take towards challenges.

Listen to the voice in your head

- If you tend to think, 'I can't …', 'Other people can …' or 'I'm useless at …', you need to change the record! Turn the message round: 'I can …', 'I have already …', 'I am going to …'

Question your way of thinking

- **Ask yourself questions such as:**
  1 Is there another way of thinking about this?
  2 Am I being a perfectionist?
  3 Am I getting things out of proportion?
  4 What can I do to improve matters?

Manage your time

Be organized

- Organize yourself to avoid stress. Make timetables and action plans to avoid predictable crises and panics.

Set priorities

- Work out your priorities and when you will do each of the tasks. Work out which things can wait — and let them.

Take care of your body

Get exercise

- Do something energetic — walk, swim, run, play a game, clean your room.

Have a healthy diet

- Check what you are putting into your body. Does your body need more substances that help it renew itself such as food and water?

Relax

Treat yourself

- Put some time aside every day just to enjoy yourself or to do nothing. Try to get at least 20 minutes on your own in the quiet.

Celebrate success

- Reflect on your achievements over the day or week — and reward yourself.

Daydream

- Imagine that you are on a magic carpet. Look down at the landscape moving beneath you. Where would you like to visit?
- Imagine that you are on a mountain top, enjoying the view.

Use a relaxation exercise

- Take time to relax, consciously.
  1 Lie on the floor or sit in a comfortable chair.
  2 Close your eyes and breathe out slowly several times. Don't force the breathing.
  3 If your mind is racing, do the 'Stop!' exercise described above.
  4 Notice where your body feels tense. Then do each of the following several times.
  5 Clench your toes tightly, count to three, then 'let go'. Repeat this several times.
  6 Repeat this with all the muscles you can, working from your toes up to your neck.
  7 Pull your shoulders right up to your ears, and let them drop. Repeat several times.
  8 Tighten all the face muscles. Then relax. Open your mouth into a big yawn.
  9 Imagine yourself in a peaceful, beautiful, safe place. Listen for sounds and look at the colors there. It can be any place, real or imaginary. This can be a safe 'retreat' in the mind for you to go when stressed.

READING	Making inferences
	Using a graphic organizer to take notes
VOCABULARY	Collocations: verb + preposition
WRITING	Using sentence variety
GRAMMAR	Object noun clauses with *that*

Discussion point

Discuss these questions with a partner.

1 Look at the photo. Why do some birds migrate?
2 What other animals migrate? What animals migrate to or from your country? Make a list.
3 What human activities can disrupt or interfere with animal movement?

Vocabulary preview

In each set of four, match the words in bold to the synonyms on the right.

1 Many animals are **adept** at making themselves invisible.   ___   **a** choose a path
2 After the overnight flight, I felt **disoriented** and jet-lagged.   ___   **b** a place to go to
3 Some fish use electrical impulses to **navigate** in deep, dark water.   ___   **c** confused
4 When we started our hike, we had no clear **destination**.   ___   **d** skilled

5 The airport closure dealt a **devastating** blow to the local economy.   ___   **e** area nearby
6 New highway construction often destroys animal **habitats**.   ___   **f** damaging
7 Scientists hope to **determine** the migratory patterns of these birds.   ___   **g** discover
8 Are there any good restaurants in the immediate **vicinity**?   ___   **h** places to live

READING 1   Invasive species you should know

Before you read

What insects do you have in your area? What problems can they cause?

Global reading

Read *Invasive species you should know*. Complete the main idea statements using phrases from the box. Then write the paragraph number.

| from South America   global trade   in the U.S.   invasive species   RIFAs |

___ **a** ALBs have been carried by cars and trucks _____.
___ **b** Red imported fire ants came to the U.S. _____.
___ **c** It's important to learn to recognize _____.
___ **d** Many invasive species are introduced into new habitats every year as a
     result of _____.
___ **e** _____ can move their colonies quickly and easily.

Close reading

█ MAKING INFERENCES

When you make an inference, you use information from a text to get (or infer) information that is not directly stated by the writer.

Often, there are no natural predators in the new area, so the species can multiply out of control, overwhelming and sometimes devastating the new environment. (You can infer that they are often hard to control or get rid of.)

Find the numbered statements in the article and ⟨circle⟩ the correct inferences you can make from them. How were you able to make those inferences?

1 That there is ___, and therefore there are too many.
   a nothing that eats this species   **b** nowhere to live

2 That invasive species are a problem ___.
   a only in some countries   **b** globally

3 That without human assistance, beetles would ___.
   a never have reached the U.S.   **b** have spread more quickly

4 That beetles are sometimes found near warehouses because ___.
   a warehouses are next to trees   **b** trucks transport crates to warehouses

5 That red imported fire ants ___ a danger to human health.
   a are   **b** are not

INVASIVE SPECIES YOU SHOULD KNOW

1 Did you know that you may have harmful foreign insects in your neighborhood? As global trade expands around the world, so do the habitats of many species of insects and plants. When products are transported from one country or continent to another, insects are often secret stowaways. Often, (1)there are no natural predators in the new area, so the species can multiply out of control, overwhelming and sometimes devastating the new environment. In other words, it becomes an invasive species. (2)Many of today's invasive species are the unfortunate result of global trade, causing millions of dollars of damage to local agriculture, vegetation, and even human health. By studying how species travel from their native habitat to a new habitat, experts can better plan for how to prevent and control invasive species. Here are two invasive species that are especially problematic in our area. Learn to recognize them!

● ASIAN LONGHORNED BEETLE (ALB)

Native habitat: China, Korea, Taiwan

Mode of transit: Wooden crates on ships from China

Invasive in: New York City (1996); Chicago (1998); Austria (2001)

Also found in: Canada, Austria, France, Italy

Characteristics: Damages hardwood trees by making holes and destroying the interior. Can be eradicated.

2 (3) Without help from humans, the Asian longhorned beetle (ALB) never moves very far or very fast. It can fly a few hundred meters, at most, and usually just stays on one tree. (4)As an invasive species, the beetles are usually first found in the vicinity of port areas and later in warehouses. Beetles often drop down from trees onto the tops of cars and trucks, and are thus transported and spread to new areas. Although the beetles have moved slowly in the U.S., their effect is devastating. In one city, more than 15,000 infected trees were cut down to control the spread. Destroying all beetles in an area is very expensive and time consuming. Many scientists are trying to determine how to get rid of this invasive beetle and prevent its spread.

● RED IMPORTED FIRE ANT (RIFA)

Native habitat: South America

Mode of transit: Soil in ships

Invasive in: Southern United States (1930s, mainly 1950s)

Also found in: Australia, Taiwan, China, and the Philippines

Characteristics: Builds mounds in fields and in urban areas; aggressive with a painful bite; can fly short distances and walk; multiplies quickly. Impossible to eradicate.

3 With a stinging bite and an appetite for anything, the red imported fire ant is an unwelcome species, wherever it lands. In the early 1950s, there was a boom in building in the U.S., resulting in an increased demand for construction materials. Ships from South America often delivered these materials, along with soil, and the ants found that this was a comfortable way to travel.

4 Because these invasive ants multiply quickly and can move their colonies, they have become a tremendous problem for homeowners, businesses, schools, and farmers. In a flood, ant 'rafts' of up to 8,000 ants can form in the water in minutes and can float for months. When it finally comes to dry land, the raft quickly comes apart as the ants climb to safety. (5)During heavy rain periods, ants will move into homes, autos, and buildings, and attack people. They are attracted to electrical currents, and cause great damage to traffic lights, air conditioners, and gas pumps.

5 Learn to recognize these invasive species and how to control them. Without natural enemies, these insects spread and cause a great deal of damage. By keeping a watchful eye on the natural world around us, we can help prevent the spread of invasive species.

Developing critical thinking

Discuss these questions in a group.

1 Compare the problems caused by the two insects. Fill in the chart. Which insect is more problematic? Why?

	Asian longhorned beetles	Red imported fire ants
How was it first transported to a new area?		
How easily can it move on its own?		
How does it affect humans?		
Are humans able to control its spread?		

2 What are some other ways that invasive species can be introduced to an area?

ACADEMIC KEYWORDS

damage	(n)	/ˈdæmɪdʒ/
natural	(adj)	/ˈnætʃ(ə)rəl/
spread	(v)	/spred/

READING 2 How do animals navigate?

Before you read

Check (✓) the different ways you think animals can navigate. Which animals use each method?

☐ smell
☐ sight
☐ sounds
☐ they remember the route

☐ they look at the sun
☐ they read the stars and moon
☐ they communicate with other animals
☐ other: _____

Global reading

1 Read *How do animals navigate?* and then discuss your *Before you read* ideas with a partner. What new information did you learn? Add it to your notes.

2 Match the information from *How do animals navigate?* to the inferences a–f. Then decide what information you can infer from number 7.

Information	Inference
___ 1 Sea turtles can read magnetic fields.	a Other species may use magnetic fields to navigate.
___ 2 Both pigeons and sea turtles read magnetic fields.	b Scientist are able to gather more accurate tracking information.
___ 3 Homing pigeons were used to carry messages.	c Scientists also use GPS to track turtles.
___ 4 Scientists are now using GPS devices to study pigeons.	d Magnetic fields can be felt through water.
___ 5 Pigeons have been disoriented by supersonic jets.	e Pigeons are not as important for sending messages as they were.
___ 6 The photo shows a turtle with a satellite tag.	f There may be other human activities that interfere with animal navigation.
7 Infrasound can be generated by ocean waves – pigeons flying over the sea got disoriented by an airplane flying over.	_____ _____

Close reading

USING A GRAPHIC ORGANIZER TO TAKE NOTES

Using a graphic organizer is an excellent way to take notes as you read. In addition, you can easily refer back to your graphic organizer to review key points or to write a summary.

Read the article again. Take notes and fill in the graphic organizer.

Sea turtle

	Where do they navigate (to/from)?	How do they navigate?
1 Sea turtles		
2 Homing pigeons		
3 Fruit bats		

How *do* animals *navigate* ?

[1] *As a young hatchling, a female sea turtle leaves the beach where she was born in search of food. As she matures, she travels great distances, perhaps even crossing vast oceans. When she reaches adulthood, she finds a mate. As the pregnant turtle prepares to lay her eggs, she is somehow drawn instinctively back, perhaps from many hundreds of miles away, to the very same beach where she herself was hatched decades earlier. How is this incredible homecoming possible?*

[2] Scientists have long been puzzled by the mysterious navigation skills of certain birds and animals. One of the most mysterious stories is that of the sea turtles. After decades of research, it is now believed that sea turtles learn and remember the particular magnetic 'address' of their birthplace, helping them return there decades later. To navigate, turtles seem to be able to 'read' the earth's magnetic field and recall the magnetic characteristics of their place of birth. Since the earth's magnetic field changes slightly over time, turtles can use information to find their way back to the area of their birthplace, but not the exact spot. Once they are in the general vicinity, turtles probably rely on sight and smell to choose the best place to lay their eggs.

[3] Another navigation genius is the homing pigeon. Moving through the sky rather than the sea, homing pigeons are famous for their ability to find their way home. They can fly hundreds of miles over unfamiliar territory without becoming disoriented. Scientists have studied homing pigeons for many years, and now with global positioning satellite (GPS) devices, they can track the exact routes that the birds take. While it has been found that pigeons may use the sight of familiar landmarks or smells, they only do this when they are near their final destination. However, pigeons seem adept at using a variety of methods for navigation. Like sea turtles, their main tools are their knowledge and memory of earth's magnetic fields. This 'map' helps them determine where they are in relation to their home.

[4] It seems that pigeons use the easiest and most reliable method in each circumstance, and are very adept at changing their navigational methods to suit the situation. A ten-year study conducted by scientists at Oxford University showed that some breeds of pigeons actually follow roads and highways, turning at intersections as they fly, even if there is a shorter way to reach their destination. Another navigational tool that pigeons may use is infrasound. These are very low frequency sounds that can travel thousands of miles and can only be heard by some animals. Infrasound can be generated by ocean waves, for example, and the constant presence of these sound waves can help pigeons figure out where they are.

[5] In 1997, a great homing pigeon race from France to England turned into a disaster when the Concorde supersonic jet flew over the flight path of the pigeons. The tremendous shock wave of sound greatly disoriented the pigeons, and only a few thousand of the 600,000 racing pigeons made it home.

Fruit bats

[6] Like pigeons, bats also use several different strategies in order to find their way around. Using tiny GPS devices, scientists conducted several different experiments to learn more about how Egyptian fruit bats navigate, and they published their results in the September 2011 issue of *Proceedings of the [US] National Academy of Sciences*. These fruit bats go out at night in search of their favorite foods, often returning to the same trees over and over again at distances of 12 to 25 kilometers from their caves. Experiments showed that bats seem to have a mental map of a large area of up to 100 kilometers, which includes familiar visual clues such as lights and hills to help them go in the right direction. The bats probably also use magnetic fields and smell when they need to, but it appears that for their regular night-time excursions they depend most heavily on their memorized maps.

ACADEMIC KEYWORDS

characteristic (n) /ˌkerəktəˈrɪstɪk/
depend (v) /dɪˈpend/
generate (v) /ˈdʒenəˌreɪt/

Developing critical thinking

1 Discuss these questions in a group.

1 Some sea turtles have been hunted for their meat and their shells for centuries. How can a better understanding of how turtles navigate help us protect these turtles?

2 Homing pigeons apparently use roads and highways to navigate. What other animals might also do this? What problems might this cause?

2 Think about the ideas from *Invasive species you should know* and *How do animals navigate?* and discuss these questions in a group.

1 Think about some other invasive creatures. How do you think they moved to new habitats? What problems do they cause?

2 How are your navigational skills? Rate your sense of direction from one to ten. Then discuss your abilities and strategies with a small group.

THINK ABOUT:

cane toads

cockroaches

common city pigeons

deer

mice

rats

termites

Vocabulary skill

COLLOCATIONS: VERB + PREPOSITION

Learning collocations is an important part of learning to speak and write English accurately. Many verbs collocate with certain prepositions, but it is hard to predict which preposition a verb will require. For this reason, it is good to learn a verb + preposition as a collocation.

*Pigeons seem **adept at** using a variety of methods for navigation.*

1 Complete the collocations with the correct preposition.

at	by	in	of	on	on	out	to

1 skilled _____

2 be drawn back _____

3 concentrate _____

4 figure _____

5 go _____ search of

6 be puzzled _____

7 rely _____

8 in search _____

2 Use the collocations in exercise 1 to complete the paragraph. You will not use all of the collocations. Change the verb form as needed.

I was recently ¹_____ a park that I loved to visit when I was a child. At first I was ²_____ this desire, but then I remembered that I had had a vivid dream about the park. So, I decided to find the park and go there. I couldn't ³_____ my memory to find the park because the last time I was there, I was only five. Also, it was in a different part of town from where I currently live. After discussing it with my older brother, I was able to ⁴_____ the general vicinity of the park. I took a bus to the area, and went ⁵_____ the park on foot. I remembered that when I was a child there were a lot of large shady trees at this park. Because I was ⁶_____ on looking for trees, I walked right by the park. I soon realized that I had just passed a playground, so I turned around. Sure enough, it was the same place. However, the lovely shade trees were all gone, replaced by playground equipment and some smaller trees.

3 Work with a partner. Discuss a time you were drawn back to a place you had known in your childhood. Describe how you found it again.

WRITING Response to an exam question

You are going to learn how to use object noun clauses, and how to use more sentence variety in your writing by using different sentence patterns. You are then going to use these to write a response to an exam question.

Writing skill

USING SENTENCE VARIETY

Using a variety of sentence types gives variation to the rhythm of your writing and makes your writing more interesting to read. Longer sentences show the reader the connection between ideas. If you tend to write only short sentences, look for ways to combine sentences as you revise your work.

Simple (one independent clause; can have two subjects or two verbs)

$$S \qquad\qquad V \qquad\qquad\qquad V$$

Destroying all beetles *in an area* is *very expensive and* takes *time.*

Compound (two independent clauses joined by a coordinating conjunction)

$$S \qquad V \qquad\qquad\qquad\qquad\qquad S \quad V$$

Pigeons may use *sight of familiar landmarks,* but they must *be near their final destination.*

Complex (an independent clause and a dependent clause)

$$S \; V \qquad\quad S \qquad V$$

If the sun is visible, pigeons will use *its location to determine true north.*

  Dep.   *Ind.*

Short sentences can also sometimes be very effective in making a point.

---

1 **Combine the short sentences into longer sentences. There are several ways to combine each pair of sentences.**

  1 He's not fluent in English. He's adept at making himself understood.
  2 My final destination is Italy. I have to fly to Zurich first.
  3 The typhoon was devastating. Many people lost their homes.
  4 An animal's habitat is destroyed by human activity. The animal must search for a new area.
  5 Costa Rica is famous for its natural beauty and unspoiled environment. Recently it has become a very popular spot for foreign tourists.

2 **Rewrite the paragraph. Revise and reword the sentences to improve sentence variety. You will not need to change every sentence.**

Some people can easily find their way in an unfamiliar place. Other people seem to get lost in their own towns. Recent studies have found genetic connections to people's ability to navigate. This may explain why some people are skillful at navigating. Some people are easily disoriented. They get lost easily. Studies show that good navigators use landmarks and streets. They orient themselves. They use visual geometry. In their heads, they visualize their location in relation to things they see around them. Researchers have found that some people with a rare genetic disease can't visually orient themselves. Experts now believe that navigational skills are inherited. They believe that some people lack certain navigation genes.

MOVEMENTUNIT 5   53

Grammar

OBJECT NOUN CLAUSES WITH *THAT*

Sometimes, when a noun clause is the object of a verb, we introduce it by the word *that*. While the word *that* is often omitted in conversation, it is usually included in academic writing.

S V   O

|I| |believe| that the |problem is very typical for new students.|

Other verbs commonly used in this kind of construction include *know*, *learn*, *show*, *determine*, and *discover*.

In formal or academic writing, the subject *it* is often used in the independent clause before the noun clause.

It is a fact / It was widely believed that ...

It has been shown that ...

It is possible/surprising/clear that ...

1 Put the words in the correct order to make sentences.

1 during / many animals / It / migration / is clear / that / great distances / travel / .

2 It / that / is / human activities / a fact / is often / interrupted by / animal migration / .

3 must migrate / It / each year / is obvious / that / fresh sources of food / many animals / to find / .

4 It / that / to the island of Hawaii / were blown / migrating nocturnal bats / was widely believed / in a storm / .

5 oil pipelines / has been shown / of caribou / that / interrupt / It / in Canada / the migration routes / .

6 that / migrate / each year / 5 billion birds / is / a fact / from / It / North to Central and South America / .

7 can fly without stopping / that / It / some migrating birds / has been reported / for 50 to 60 hours / .

2 Complete the sentences with the words in the box or your own ideas.

airplanes	cars	GPS devices	transportation	urban bicyclists

1 It is a fact that _____

2 It is obvious that_____

3 It is believed that_____

4 It has been shown that _____

5 It is possible that in the future _____

WRITING TASK

Write a response paragraph to an exam question on either invasive species or animal movement.

Audience: teacher
Context: examination question
Purpose: to answer an examination question by writing a paragraph

BRAINSTORM

1 Read the exam question and a student's response. Then answer these questions.

  1 How many pieces of information should be in the answer? What information did the writer *not* include?

  2 Find and underline the two noun clauses with *that*.

  3 Does the paragraph have sentence variety? How many very short sentences are there?

> *Exam question: Research an invasive species. Write a paragraph telling where it came from, how it came to the new area, why the habitat is suitable for it, and why it is a problem. Include information on how it can be controlled.*
>
> The kudzu is an invasive species of plant that has spread across a great deal of the southern United States. It first arrived in the United States as part of a plant exhibition from Japan in 1876. Due to its beautiful leaves and fragrant flowers, it was very popular and people were enthusiastic about planting it in their cities, towns, and yards. Everyone wanted this unusual, easy to grow plant. The problem was that it grew too fast. It spread out of control. People soon discovered that the kudzu vine could cover a hillside or a small house in a few months. The kudzu covers and kills other plants and trees. Unfortunately, this invasive plant seems impossible to destroy. The current control methods include frequent cutting, digging out the roots, applying chemicals, and even having goats eat the plants.

2 Read the two exam questions, and choose *one* to answer. Choose a topic to research.

> *Exam question 1: Answer the question in the example above. Suggested topics: corn borer, cane toads, or zebra mussels.*

> *Exam question 2: Research how a specific animal or insect navigates. Discuss how it moves and how it can navigate. Include information about research, if possible. You may wish to point out similarities to the sea turtle or the homing pigeon. Suggested topics: salmon, monarch butterflies, or whales.*

salmon

monarch butterfly

whale

corn borer moth

zebra mussel

PLAN

Plan your paragraph. Make an outline of the information you want to include. Check that you will have answered the question completely.

WRITE

Write a paragraph in response to the exam question. Make sure you use topic sentences and include supporting details. Include several noun clauses with *that*, and if possible, vocabulary from the unit.

SHARE

Exchange paragraphs with a partner. Read the checklist on page 109 and provide feedback to your partner.

REWRITE AND EDIT

Consider your partner's comments and write a final draft of your response. Check that you have a variety of sentence patterns.

STUDY SKILLS   Strategies for writing timed essays

Getting started

Discuss these questions with a partner.

1 Have you ever done any timed writing (writing which you were given a time limit to complete)? How did you feel about it?

2 For you, what is most challenging about timed writing? Check three things.

☐ deciding what to write   ☐ expressing my ideas clearly in writing

☐ organizing my ideas   ☐ not having time to revise my work

☐ feeling nervous or stressed   ☐ using correct spelling and grammar

☐ finishing on time

3 Look at the three challenges you checked above. For each one, think of an idea that would help make it easier for you.

Scenario

Read this scenario and think about what Jun Ho is doing right and what he is doing wrong.

Consider it

Look at these tips for timed writing. Which ones do you think would be easy to follow? Which could be more challenging for you? Why?

1 **Plan your time carefully** Leave time for planning, writing, and revising. For example, for a 45-minute essay, take 10 minutes for planning, 25 minutes for writing, and 10 minutes for revising.

2 **Analyze the essay question (prompt)** You will lose points on your essay if you do not answer the question, or if your response is incomplete. Read the prompt two or three times and underline the key words.

3 **Identify your main idea** Once you understand the prompt question, write a sentence that answers it and tells how you will support your answer in your essay, for example, *There should be stricter laws against texting while driving, in particular for teen drivers, in busy downtown areas, and on major highways.* This is your *thesis statement* and should be in your introduction.

4 **Gather and organize main points and supporting ideas** Make a brief outline and include only points that relate directly to your thesis.

5 **Write** Refer to your outline regularly. Add new ideas if they relate to your thesis. However, do not try to write as much as possible. How much you write is not as important as how well you answer the question.

6 **Read and revise** Check that all of the sentences in your essay relate back to your thesis. Read each sentence and correct any errors. Add transitions (e.g. *in addition, however*) to help clarify and organize your ideas. If you want to add any points on a handwritten essay, write neatly in the margin and draw an arrow to show where they should be inserted.

Over to you

Discuss these questions with a partner.

1 What could you do to avoid feeling nervous in timed essay situations?

2 Which tips are the most important for you?

3 The next time you do timed writing, what will you do differently? Which tips above will you try?

Jun Ho is taking an English composition class. To help students practice for tests, the teacher often assigns timed essays in class. Students are given a question and have 45 minutes to write an essay about it, for example, expressing an opinion about a current topic. Jun Ho finds it challenging to write quickly and is often nervous that he will not have enough time to finish, so he reads the question once and starts writing his introduction immediately. As he writes the body paragraphs of his essay, he tries to include examples or details to support his opinion. He continues writing as much as possible, as quickly as possible, without stopping because he wants to make sure he does not miss any important ideas. He leaves at least two or three minutes at the end to check his work and correct his spelling and grammar. When he gets his paper back, his teacher comments that his essay lacks organization, that he has included details that are not relevant, and that not all of his points are well supported.

Disease

READING	Increasing reading speed
	Distinguishing fact from opinion
VOCABULARY	Words with Greek and Latin origins
WRITING	Thesis statements
GRAMMAR	Passive modals: advice, ability, and possibility

Discussion point

Discuss these questions with a partner.

1 How have medical technology and treatment changed since your grandparents were young? What about your parents? How have they changed in your lifetime?

2 What are some interesting or amazing uses of technology in modern medicine? List as many as you can.

3 What types of medical advances do you think, or hope, the future will bring?

Vocabulary preview

Complete the sentences with the words in the box.

> applications   diagnosis   disorders   genetic
> precise   resolve   symptoms   widespread

1 The nurse explained the _____ details of the surgery.
2 I hope this medication will finally _____ my headaches.
3 The use of herbal medicines is becoming more _____ these days.
4 Pain relief is just one _____ of the drug, aspirin.
5 Sometimes tests are needed before a doctor can make a clear _____.
6 The _____ of a cold can include fever and loss of appetite.
7 Some allergies are _____. My mother and I are both allergic to nuts.
8 Research has shown that eating _____ amongst men are on the increase.

READING 1 Long-distance care

Before you read

Work with a partner. In recent years, many types of jobs have become automated. What are the pros and cons of this increased reliance on robots?

Global reading

INCREASING READING SPEED

Learning to read faster is a useful skill for academic texts, as well as for taking tests. Here are four useful strategies

1 Preview the text. Look at the title and any headings, images, and graphics.

2 Use your finger or pen to help guide your eyes faster across the text.

3 Don't read every word. Focus on content words—usually nouns and verbs—that carry the main meaning in the text.

4 Adjust your reading speed according to what you need from the text.

THINK ABOUT:

communication   medicine
employment   transport
entertainment   travel

1 **Take one minute to read *Long-distance care* on the next page. Read as much as you can and mark where you finish. Then complete the chart with as much information as you can about these points.**

A definition of telesurgery:	Advantages:
History:	The future of telesurgery:

2 **Read the whole article and complete the chart in exercise 1.**

Close reading

Complete the missing information in the summary of *Long-distance care.*

Telesurgery is a type of surgery that can be performed [1] _____
_____ .

The surgeon uses [2] _____
_____
to send instructions to a set of robotic arms, which perform the surgery. The patient may never be
[3] _____ .

Telesurgery allows doctors to operate in areas [4] _____
_____ . Some studies have shown that for some types of operations,
robot-performed surgery is [5] _____ than traditional surgery. In the
future, telesurgery may be used for many applications including, [6] _____
_____ .

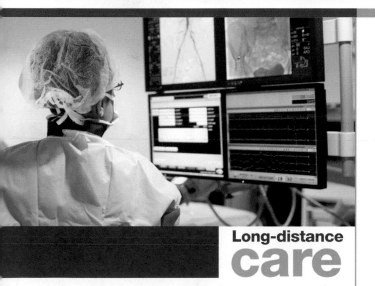

Long-distance
care

What is telesurgery?

[1] Imagine a hospital operating room. A patient lies on an operating table under bright, white lights. High-tech monitors around the room beep and buzz, measuring oxygen intake, heart rate, and blood pressure. Doctors and nurses in white coats stand, masked and gloved, ready for instructions. There's only one person missing, the surgeon, who is, in this case, performing the operation from a different hospital thousands of kilometers away. This is telesurgery, also called remote surgery, a practice that someday might be used more often than traditional surgery for some types of operations. From the Greek word *tele*, meaning 'far off' and *cheirourgia*, meaning 'working by hand', telesurgery is an operation that can be performed by a surgeon at a site far removed from the patient's location. The surgeon's precise instructions can be delivered to a set of robotic arms through a complex system of high speed Internet connections and fiber-optic cables. The robotic arms perform the surgery from beginning to end, and the patient may never even be touched by a doctor's hands.

Current applications

[2] Many people may feel that a robot cannot be trusted to do the job of a highly-trained surgeon. However, while the advantages of remote surgery may not be immediately clear, the amazing possibilities should be noted. Consider the lives that can be saved when doctors can operate in areas where access to expert or specialized medical care may be limited, or where travel to a larger hospital is difficult. Another surprising advantage of robot-performed surgery is accuracy. A study conducted at Guy's Hospital in London, England found that, in 304 cases of kidney surgeries on dummy patients, those conducted using robots more accurately targeted kidney stones.

History and research

[3] One of the first telesurgeries was performed in 2001. From a hospital in New York City, Dr. Jacques Marescaux conducted a gall bladder removal operation on a 68-year-old female patient 6,230 kilometers away in Strasbourg, France. Since then, continual advances in technology have allowed for the practice to become more widespread.

Toward the future

[4] Research is being conducted to learn the potential range of applications for telesurgery for the future, including training surgeons in developing countries, treating injured soldiers on the battlefield, and even conducting surgical procedures in space. Of course, like so many things, the fine points of telesurgery could be improved. Depending on the distance the information has to travel, the reaction time of the robotic arms can be delayed slightly, and computer compatibility can be an issue as well. However, as technology continues to advance, these issues can certainly be resolved, allowing doctors to provide expert medical care to patients around the globe, hands-free.

ACADEMIC KEYWORDS		
advance	(n)	/ədˈvæns/
practice	(n)	/ˈpræktɪs/
procedure	(n)	/prəˈsidʒər/

Developing critical thinking

Discuss these questions in a group.

1 What do you think the author's views of telesurgery are? Are they in favor of it? How do you know?

2 Compare and contrast traditional surgery and telesurgery. Make a list of similarities and differences between the two practices. Then discuss the advantages and disadvantages of each for the doctor and for the patient.

THINK ABOUT:

accuracy   cost
convenience   timing

READING 2 Do we know too much?

Before you read

Work with a partner. What are some of your own genetic traits that you feel came from your mother's side of the family? What about your father's?

Global reading

Read *Do we know too much?* quickly. Follow the guidelines for increasing reading speed on page 58. Then work with a partner to answer these questions.

1 Who is currently helped by genetic testing?

2 How many different ways of using genetic testing are listed here?

3 Name two examples of genetic material that can be used.

4 Name two examples of how genetic testing is used outside of medicine.

THINK ABOUT:

abilities
appearance
eyesight
height
likes
personality

Close reading

DISTINGUISHING FACT FROM OPINION

It's important to recognize the difference between facts and the author's opinions, especially when you are reading a text for academic research.

A **fact** can be observed, proven, measured, or shown with numbers or statistics.

An **opinion** often uses adjectives or adverbs to express a personal judgment. *Unfortunately, far too many Americans are without health insurance.*

Sometimes a statement may include both a fact and an opinion.

A shocking 16.3% of Americans are without health insurance.

Opinions can be supportable (i.e. we can back them up with evidence), or unsupportable (more subjective). Note that some opinions are presented as if they were facts. We need to learn to read critically to make the distinction between what is a fact and what is an author's opinion.

More than any other scientific development this century, genetic testing has the power to lengthen and improve people's lives. (presented as a fact, but is actually an opinion)

Read *Do we know too much?* again. Are the numbered statements F (facts) or O (opinions)? Work with a partner to discuss your reasons.

1 ___   4 ___
2 ___   5 ___
3 ___   6 ___

ACADEMIC KEYWORDS

development (n) /dɪˈveləpmənt/
opportunity (n) /ˌɑpərˈtunəti/
risk   (n) /rɪsk/

Do we *know* too much?

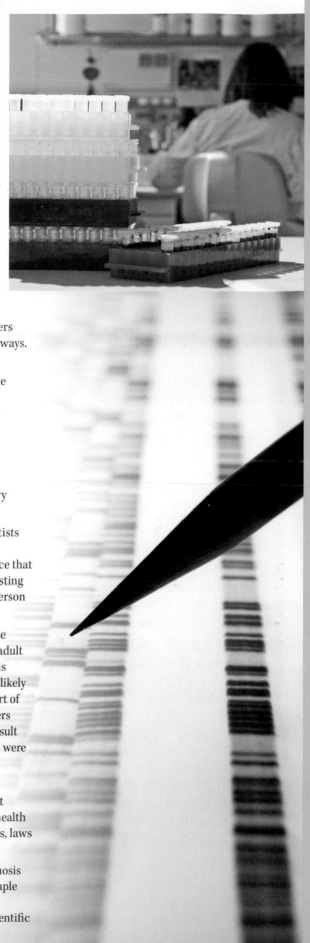

Recent advances in medical technology have allowed for lightning-fast diagnosis, more effective treatments, and even cures for many types of diseases. But what if there was a way to prevent some diseases from ever starting in the first place? Genetic testing offers a unique opportunity to find hidden diseases in our genes before they start, so we can take action to prevent them.

Genetic tests (also known as DNA-based tests) can be used to determine how likely a person is to develop a genetic disorder later in life. They are also used with patients who are displaying symptoms of diseases or who have already been diagnosed with certain diseases. [1]This is truly one of the most amazing advances in medical history.

[2]Currently more than 1,000 genetic tests are available for a range of disorders from allergies to cancer. Genetic tests may be used in a variety of different ways. Applications include:

- Newborn screening – to identify disorders that are treatable early in the child's life.

- Diagnostic testing – in order to confirm or rule out the presence of a particular disease.

- Carrier testing – used to determine whether a person carries a genetic disorder which could be passed down to his or her children.

- Predictive testing – to predict a person's risk for developing a hereditary disease later in life.

[3]The testing process is fascinating and complex. To perform the test, scientists examine genetic material, for example, in a piece of hair, or from inside a person's mouth. They look for abnormalities in the DNA pattern or sequence that show signs of a particular disease. If an abnormality is detected, further testing and a precise analysis of other factors can help determine how likely the person is to eventually develop the disease.

[4]These tests provide an exciting opportunity that should not be ignored: the chance to lead a healthier life and avoid certain diseases. For example, an adult male who has a family history of heart disease can take a test to find out his own chances of contracting the same disease. If the test results show he is likely to develop the disease, certain measures may be taken to postpone the start of the disease. [5]In a recent study at Johns Hopkins University, 58% of test takers said they learned information that would improve their health, and as a result of testing, 34% said they were being more careful about their diet, and 14% were exercising more.

Of course, not all aspects of genetic testing are positive. Patients may feel stressed or confused about test results and may not know what to do about them. In addition, some people worry about problems with employers or health insurance companies if their test results become public. In many U.S. states, laws have been passed to protect people and keep test results private.

The applications of genetic testing are widespread. In addition to the diagnosis of diseases, tests can be used to research a person's family history, for example to find lost relatives, or to trace family ancestry. [6]Police are also using the technology to identify criminals and solve crimes. More than any other scientific development this century, genetic testing has the power to lengthen and improve people's lives.

Developing critical thinking

1 Discuss these questions in a group.

1 List both the positive and negative aspects of genetic testing described in *Do we know too much?* Which aspects does the author focus on more? Can you list any other possible pros and cons?

2 Look at the four types of genetic testing listed in *Do we know too much?* How might each type affect people's decisions or actions?

2 Think about the ideas from *Long-distance care* and *Do we know too much?* and discuss these questions in a group.

1 Are all advances in science and technology good for humankind? Why or why not? Give examples.

2 What might be some long-term consequences of so many medical developments that continue to extend humans' lives?

Vocabulary skill

WORDS WITH GREEK AND LATIN ORIGINS

Like other sciences, the field of medicine uses many words that originate from Greek (such as *tele*) or Latin. These word parts are common throughout English vocabulary. Studying their meaning can help you expand your vocabulary and guess the meaning of unknown words.

Greek: **anti**anxiety, **auto**biography, **cardio**logist, **neuro**logical, **psycho**analyst

Latin: **ambi**guous, **cerebra**l, **opti**cian

1 Match the prefixes with their meanings a–h. Use the words in the vocabulary skill box to help.

Origin		Meaning	
1	ambi- ___	a	self
2	anti- ___	b	relating to the heart
3	auto- ___	c	both sides
4	cardio- ___	d	against; opposing
5	cerebro- ___	e	relating to the eyes
6	neuro- ___	f	relating to the brain
7	optic- ___	g	relating to the nerves
8	psych- ___	h	relating to the mind

2 Complete the sentences using the words from the Vocabulary skill box.

1 That movie was too _____ for me. I prefer films that don't require so much mental effort.

2 This _____ has performed over 100 successful heart surgeries.

3 Jim has problems sleeping when he is stressed. He has been trying to resolve it with _____ medication.

4 His explanation was _____. It could have had two meanings.

5 You should really see an _____. I think you need glasses.

6 I'm reading the _____ of Nobel Prize-winning Doctor Joseph Murray. He wrote it in 1990.

7 I'm interested in how the mind works. I think I'd like to be a _____.

8 The patient had a brain scan to determine whether or not the symptoms had a _____ cause.

WRITING Persuasive essay: A health recommendation

You are going to learn about thesis statements and supporting sentences, and using modals for advice, ability, and possibility. You are then going to use these to write an essay making recommendations to prevent disease and improve people's health, and persuade readers to agree with your opinion.

Writing skill

THESIS STATEMENTS

A thesis statement is a sentence that appears in the introductory paragraph of an essay, usually as the last sentence of the paragraph. It is like a GPS, letting the reader know where you plan to take them. The rest of your essay should support the thesis statement.

A good thesis statement should explain the **main point** of your essay, your **opinion** of it, and how you plan to **support** it in the essay.

The best ways to stay healthy and prevent disease are to follow a good diet, exercise regularly, and get regular physical exams.

1 **Read the paragraph below and choose the best thesis statement to complete it.**

  a In a recent survey, over 40% of young people aged 15–18 said they spent more than five hours per day in front of a computer.

  b In order to avoid becoming an unhealthy society, we must increase the focus on sports in schools, and educate young people about the health risks of an inactive lifestyle.

  c Local and national governments should take immediate action to protect the health of future generations.

In today's technology-focused society, many young people are spending more time sitting in front of their computers, staying indoors for many hours, eating a lot of unhealthy snacks, and drinking high-calorie sweet drinks. They're also spending less time doing activities that keep them fit and healthy. As a result, young people have more weight problems and, over time, serious issues like heart disease may develop.

2 **Read these statements. Check (✓) the three sentences that are good thesis statements.**

  ☐ **1** Most people choose not to have predictive genetic testing.

  ☐ **2** Stress is one of the leading causes of heart problems.

  ☐ **3** Many health problems can be avoided if people get enough sleep and take steps to reduce stress.

  ☐ **4** Employers only offer health insurance to full-time employees.

  ☐ **5** Older adults should consider the health benefits of switching to a vegetarian diet, including weight loss and a lower risk of heart disease.

  ☐ **6** The most important step in preventing disease in later life is for parents to encourage their children to eat more fresh fruits and vegetables, and fewer sugary, fatty junk foods.

  ☐ **7** Telesurgery procedures are still not covered by most insurance companies.

  ☐ **8** A vegetarian diet has both advantages and disadvantages.

3 **Rewrite the other five facts in exercise 2 as good thesis statements.**

Grammar

PASSIVE MODALS: ADVICE, ABILITY, AND POSSIBILITY

Should, can/could, and *may/might* are modals. Passive modals are formed with modal + *be* + past participle of the verb. Note that in the passive form, the object of the sentence becomes the subject, and the original subject is sometimes omitted.	*People can't change bad health habits easily.* → *Bad health habits* **can't be changed** *easily.*
Should is used to give advice or make recommendations.	*Young people* **should be encouraged** *to participate in sports.*
Can and *could* express ability.	*Many diseases* **can be prevented***. Consider the lives that* **could be saved***.*
Could can also express future possibility.	*A cure for cancer* **could be found** *within the next decade.*
May and *might* express present and future possibility.	*Telesurgery* **might be used** *more frequently in the future. The patient* **may** *never even* **be touched** *by a doctor's hands.*

1 Read the sentences from *Long-distance care* and *Do we know too much?* Check (✓) the correct type of modal for each one.

		Advice	Ability	Possibility
1	In the future, telesurgery **might be used** more often than traditional surgery.			
2	Telesurgery **can be performed** by a surgeon at a site far removed from the patient.			
3	However, while the advantages of remote surgery may not be immediately clear, the amazing possibilities **should be noted**.			
4	If the test results show a person is likely to develop a disease, certain measures **may be taken** to postpone the start of the disease.			
5	In addition to the diagnosis of diseases, tests **can be used** to research a person's family history.			

2 Rewrite these sentences using passive modals. Leave the subject out where it isn't necessary.

1 We might prevent all diseases someday.
2 People should consider the risks of an inactive lifestyle.
3 People can reduce stress if they make time to do the things they enjoy.
4 Children can learn good health habits from an early age.
5 People should only take genetic tests for treatable diseases.
6 People should consult a doctor about any health concerns.
7 Older people can improve their memory if they walk.

3 Add three more statements using the passive modals, to express your views about health and medicine.

WRITING TASK

Write a persuasive essay. Give advice or make a recommendation to help people lead a healthier life.

Audience:	classmates/peers
Context:	an essay persuading people to make changes to improve their health
Purpose:	to use details and examples to support an opinion or recommendation

BRAINSTORM

Choose from the following health-related topic ideas, or use your own idea. Make a list of specific actions that people can take to prevent disease or improve their overall health.

- Changing a habit (caffeine, smoking, etc.)
- Diet/Nutrition
- Fitness/Exercise
- Genetic tests
- Rest/Sleep
- Stress reduction

PLAN

Plan your thesis statement for your essay. What information or examples will you include to support it? Write a sentence that explains your main point, your opinion of it, and how you plan to support it in the essay. Then list details and examples you can use to support your thesis. Check that all of them relate to your thesis statement.

Thesis statement: _____

_____

Supporting details and examples: _____

_____

WRITE

Write a three-paragraph persuasive essay about your chosen health-related topic and including advice on the topic.

1 In the first paragraph: Describe the health issue and your advice. Include a thesis statement that explains your opinion and how you will support it.

2 In the second paragraph, give reasons and examples to support your advice.

3 In the final paragraph, write a conclusion that summarizes the issue and your advice.

Use passive modals to give advice, express ability, and express future possibility.

SHARE

Exchange papers with a partner. Is there a clear thesis statement? Do all of the rest of the sentences relate to it? Did the writer use passive modals correctly? Use the checklist on page 109.

REWRITE AND EDIT

Consider your partner's comments and rewrite your essay.

STUDY SKILLS Participating in online discussion boards

Getting started

Discuss these questions with a partner.

1 Have you ever used an online discussion board? How did you feel about it?
2 Would you prefer a class discussion or an online discussion? Why?

Scenario

Read this scenario and think about what Fatima did right and what she did wrong.

Consider it

Read the tips about participating in online discussion boards. Discuss each one with a partner. Which tips are most useful to you?

1 **Read instructions and grading rubric carefully** Your instructor will provide instructions about how to participate in the online discussion board. For most courses, your participation will be graded, so read the instructor's grading rubric carefully to see what is expected. Follow the guidelines very carefully.

2 **Use a formal writing style** A discussion board is not a chat room, where people write quickly and in a conversational style. Your responses should be carefully written. Do not use abbreviations, slang, or emoticons ☺.

3 **Respond, explain, and quote** This formula may work well for your course if you are being asked to respond to a question or to something that you have read. Start by giving your opinion or response, explain it with an example, and then back up your point with a quote from the reading.

4 **Stay on topic** Make sure your comment is directly related to the topic and that you are including your insight into the topic.

5 **Review before you post** Always check your post for spelling and grammar errors before posting it. Also make sure that your tone is polite and respectful of others.

6 **Respond thoughtfully** Your instructor is not looking for a summary of what you have read or a note that just says you agree or disagree. Your instructor wants your thoughtful responses, offering your opinions and insights that are related to the topic or question. If you are responding to a classmate's post, explain why you do or do not agree and include additional information.

Over to you

Discuss these questions with a partner.

1 Why are academic writing skills important for an online discussion board?
2 How do you think an online discussion board might improve your learning in a course?

Fatima enrolled in a history class at her university, and the instructor required students to participate in an online discussion board. The instructor would post a question about the reading assignment, and students had three days to post a response online. Fatima writes a lot of texts and emails, so she thought this would be easy to do. For the first discussion question, she read one student's post and then wrote this response: 'u r so right. i totally agree.' Fatima was embarrassed in the next class when the instructor mentioned her response and told students that they needed to use appropriate writing style for a college course. The instructor explained that students needed to offer their own insights and make references to what they read. After that, Fatima went to the online guidelines for the discussion board that the instructor had posted. After reading them, she had a much better idea of what was expected. However, she was still shy about posting her comments because she wasn't confident about her academic writing style.

READING	Using questions to be an active reader
	Annotating text
VOCABULARY	Prefixes *un-* and *in-*
WRITING	Writing about cause and effect
GRAMMAR	Unreal conditional in the past

Discussion point

Discuss these questions with a partner.

1 Describe a geographical place where survival is difficult. Have you ever been in such a place?

2 What makes survival so difficult there?

3 What would you need to have to survive there? Make a list and circle the two most important things.

Vocabulary preview

Read the sentences. Then circle the word or phrase that is closest in meaning to the word in bold.

1 The book about the expedition was **converted** into an e-book.
   a changed   **b** substituted

2 Staying hydrated is **critical** to survival in both hot and cold conditions.
   a difficult   **b** extremely important

3 Without any tools, my father **devised** a way to fix the motorboat.
   a invented a way of doing something   **b** made a decision about

4 He felt frozen because the thin shirt didn't **insulate** him from the cold.
   a prevent cold from passing through   **b** encourage heat production

5 After the rainstorm, we discovered **moisture** inside the tent.
   a hot air   **b** a small amount of water

6 The high winds **prevented** the captain from turning the ship.
   a put into danger   **b** stopped from doing

7 Since it is a long hike, hikers should carry **sufficient** food and water.
   a as much as will be needed   **b** very nutritious

8 An ice storm results in **treacherous** driving conditions.
   a extremely strong   **b** extremely dangerous

READING 1 *Adrift*: A book report

Before you read

Before reading *Adrift: A book report*, predict what kinds of information will be included in the report. Make a list. Then compare your list with a partner.

Global reading

■ USING QUESTIONS TO BE AN ACTIVE READER ■

Keeping questions in mind will help you bring a more focused approach to your reading. Here are four ways to use questions to be an active reader:

1 You can use questions to think about your purpose for reading the text or article. What information do you need?

2 Before you read, you can write down three questions that you have about the topic, and keep the questions in mind as you read.

3 You can read the comprehension questions that come with the reading. Select several questions to use for active reading.

4 As you read, next to every paragraph, you can write one question that you have about what you have read.

1 **Read these questions and add one question of your own. Then read *Adrift: A book report*, keeping the questions in mind.**

   1 What is the book title, author, and publication date?
   2 Is the book fiction or non-fiction?
   3 Why did the writer choose this book to read?
   4 What is the story about? Where does the story take place?
   5 Does the writer like the book? Why or why not?
   6 _____

2 **Write two sentences to summarize what the book is about.**

Close reading

Complete the notes on *Adrift: A book report*. Then make notes on paragraphs 4 and 5.

Paragraph 1
- *writer likes to read about* [1] _____ *experiences and survival stories*
- [2] _____: *story of one man's* [3] _____ *at sea.*

Paragraph 2
- *sails from Penzance,* [4] _____ *in a race*
- *Callahan is very* [5] _____, *very* [6] _____
- *ship hits* [7] _____ *and* [8] _____

Paragraph 3
- [9] _____ *days aboard* [10] _____
- *converts* [11] _____ *water into* [12] _____ *water*
- *keeps notes about* [13] _____, *water, and* [14] _____

Developing critical thinking

Discuss these questions in a group.

1 Few people have survived more than a few weeks in an inflatable raft. How important do you think Callahan's attitude and survival tactics were to his survival for over ten weeks? Give reasons.

2 Why do you think we like to read books or watch shows about people who survive treacherous situations?

ACADEMIC KEYWORDS

account	(n)	/əˈkaʊnt/
critical	(adj)	/ˈkrɪtɪk(ə)l/
detailed	(adj)	/dɪˈteɪld/

Adrift: A book report

[1] Like many people, I have always been fascinated with the question of how individuals are able to survive under life-threatening conditions. But rather than watching reality TV shows about 'survival' or dramatic movies, I prefer reading first-person accounts of real experiences. *Adrift: Seventy-Six Days Lost at Sea* by Steven Callahan (1986, Houghton Mifflin, Harcourt) is a truly amazing story of one man's survival at sea.

[2] In 1982 Callahan sets out from Penzance, England in a solo transatlantic race, sailing across the Atlantic to Antigua in the Caribbean Islands. A very experienced sailor and boatbuilder, Callahan is as prepared for disaster as any sailor could be. But one dark night, when his boat hits a very large object (probably a whale), he has less than a minute to abandon his sinking ship, struggling to pull loose the life raft and grab whatever supplies he can.

[3] *Adrift* tells the true story of Callahan's life for 76 days onboard his small inflatable raft. Even though he is in shock at having lost his sailboat, from the first day on the raft, Callahan carefully evaluates his situation. He estimates where he is, what direction he is traveling in, and where he might come across ships that could rescue him. He only has a few bottles of fresh water, and realizes that his most critical task is to devise a solar still — a small device to collect salt water and convert it into drinking water using the sun. Using a small notepad, he keeps a daily log, noting what he drank, ate, and did, and how much he exercised. This allowed him to measure his physical and mental state, and restrict his food and water.

[4] As a reader, you experience his mental struggle as he strives to remain calm and positive, determined to solve each small disaster that threatens his very survival. He suffers from lack of shelter as he is exposed to relentless sun during the day, extreme cold at night, salt water and moisture. As days turn into weeks, he battles intense hunger, loneliness, and the deterioration of his body and mind. His tactics for survival, from doing daily yoga to stay strong to having an imaginary captain order him to do things, are impressive. His self-control helps him maintain his sanity. What I found amazing about this story was Callahan's ability to come up with solutions to the endless problems that arise. He has to constantly repair his spear for fishing and his still for collecting drinking water, or he faces certain death.

[5] Through the 76 treacherous days alone on the ocean, you feel Callahan's despair, his hope, his determination, and his connection with the little signs of life around him. Callahan's vivid writing style and detailed account of his ordeal, accompanied by his own drawings, bring his frightening experience alive in his book. His strength of spirit, knowledge, and know-how carry him through this nightmare. In our modern day and age, such a person is rare, which makes reading this book an unforgettable experience.

READING 2 A semester on ice

Before you read

Take this quiz to test your knowledge about Antarctica. Circle the correct word and then discuss with a partner.

1 Antarctica is a **country** / **continent**.
2 It is near the **North** / **South** Pole.
3 The **winter** / **summer** months are December, January, February, when the sun **always** / **never** shines.
4 It is about 1.5 times the size of **the USA** / **the United Kingdom**.
5 It has the most **predictable** / **dangerous** weather in the entire world.

Global reading

Read *A semester on ice* and answer the questions.

1 What is hypothermia?
2 What are the four keys to survival in Antarctica?
3 Which questions in *Before you read* are answered in the blog?
4 Why do you think the survival training is required?

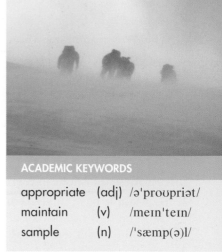

ACADEMIC KEYWORDS

appropriate	(adj)	/əˈprəʊpriət/
maintain	(v)	/meɪnˈteɪn/
sample	(n)	/ˈsæmp(ə)l/

Close reading

ANNOTATING TEXT

Annotating text involves adding notes to it or underlining parts of it, to help you understand what you read and assist you in finding key information later. It's best to annotate during your second reading of the text. There are several ways to annotate text.

1 Underline or highlight key phrases or facts.
2 After you read each paragraph, write a few words in the margin to describe the topic of the paragraph.
3 Reread the text and write questions that you have. Start your questions with 'Why?' Later, you can discuss these questions and perhaps look for answers elsewhere.

Match the annotation notes a–g with paragraphs 1–7.

a *What they learned at camp*   ___
b *Importance of survival training, now and in the future* ___
c *Being prepared* ___
d *Packing bags* ___
e *4 keys to survival* ___
f *Day 2: definition of hypothermia* ___
g *Hypothermia and confusion* ___

Developing critical thinking

1 **Discuss these questions in a group.**

1 What types of research take place in Antarctica? Why is this research important? Which type of research are you interested in, and why?
2 Kamal chose to spend three months in Antarctica, the coldest place on the earth. In spite of the challenges, how do you think he benefited from this experience?

THINK ABOUT:

climate change	technology
geology	weather
physiology	wildlife

Blog: A semester on ice

Kamal Osman

About me: *I'm a geosciences doctoral student from Turkey, and I am spending three months at the Western Antarctic Ice Sheet (WAIS) research station near McMurdo Station. There, I will be helping an international team of researchers collect a three kilometer deep ice sample. In this blog, I'll be writing about daily life and my research down here near the South Pole.*

Posted December 12

[1] I've just completed day 2 in Antarctica, but I was inside almost all day here at McMurdo Station. We are in the summer months (December, January, February) with an average temperature of about –3 °C (26.6°F) and almost 24 hours of daylight. This morning I attended the required training on safety and survival. We spent much of the time discussing hypothermia, when the body temperature drops well below normal to 35 °C (95 °F) or lower, leading to a chain of events that can result in death.

[2] Staying warm is essential to living down here, and maintaining body temperature is critical. If your body temperature drops even a few degrees, you can develop hypothermia. One of the early symptoms of hypothermia is the inability to think clearly, which leads to a person making bad decisions. Owing to the mental confusion of hypothermia, a person doesn't realize what is happening or what to do. At the first signs of confusion in another person, you must act quickly to increase the person's body temperature. In our training, we learned how to wrap a person in a sleeping bag, covering the head with a wool hat to prevent the loss of body heat. (Did you know that you can lose 20–30% of your body heat through your head?) Working in these treacherous conditions is all about being prepared and knowing the signs of hypothermia.

[3] Altogether there are four keys to survival: lots of clothing, shelter from the weather and moisture, appropriate and sufficient food, and water. All of these help you maintain body temperature. As you can see from my photo, I wear many layers of special clothing to insulate me and to trap body heat. For emergency shelter from wind and snow, we will learn how to dig a survival trench in the snow — useful if you don't have a tent. Sufficient water isn't a problem here. Over 70% of the earth's water is here. It's just that it is frozen! Finally, you must have the right kind of food. This is the part I love about being here — I have to eat lots! In mild weather conditions, the body only spends about half of its food energy to maintain body temperature. However, in Antarctica, almost all of the energy generated by the food you eat goes to keeping you warm. For this reason, we must eat large quantities of high-calorie foods. You body can quickly convert these foods into energy.

[4] This afternoon, we packed our bags for the overnight training trip tomorrow, and I included lots extra clothing and lots of high-energy foods! I guess chocolate bars aren't so bad for you after all!

Posted December 14

[5] I've just gotten back to McMurdo Station, after two days of the required 'Happy Camper School'. The name suggests that it's a lot of fun, but actually this training is all about survival in an emergency situation. Before leaving, the instructors checked our extra clothing because the weather here can quickly become life-threatening. That's one of the first lessons they stressed: always be prepared, and always let others know of your travel plans. If you don't show up at the expected time, people will know that you are in trouble.

[6] Fortunately, during our two days at the remote camp, the weather wasn't too cold (around 3.6°C high and –6.8°C low), but the wind was blowing, making it feel much colder. We learned how to build a wind protection wall out of snow blocks, how to dig a snow trench to sleep in, how to pitch a tent and use a camping stove, and once again, how to avoid hypothermia. Our instructors left us on our own in the evening to test our survival skills. It was exhausting work, and I hardly slept at night due to the howling wind.

[7] During the camp, I could see how important my survival training was. One mistake could start a chain reaction of bad events, endangering yourself and others. When our second day of training was over, we sat exhausted on our backpacks, awaiting the arrival of our instructors to transport us 'home' to the warmth of McMurdo Station, to hot meals and warm showers. I know that the training will be invaluable as I work in Antarctica, but I also think that the lessons I learned about safety, staying warm, and how to take care of myself will stay with me the rest of my life.

2 Think about the ideas from *Adrift: A book report* and *A semester on ice* and discuss these questions in a group.

1 Think about the four keys to survival in *A semester on ice*. Then make notes how Callahan in *Adrift* addressed these challenges. You may need to make inferences if the information is not directly stated in the text.

clothing and insulation — I can infer that his clothing didn't protect him from the sun, heat, cold, and moisture.

2 How would you prepare for each situation? Make a list of what you would need and explain the reason for each item.
- cycling trip through the desert
- car trip during winter
- car trip during summer
- camping trip in the mountains

Vocabulary skill

PREFIXES *UN-* AND *IN-*

Recognizing and understanding prefixes is a good way to expand your vocabulary. The prefixes *un-* and *in-* are often added to adjectives, changing the meaning to *not* or *the opposite of*: *correct — incorrect, usual — unusual.*

If a word starts with *m* or *p*, you may use **im-**: *possible = impossible*

If a word starts with *r*, you may use **ir-**: *responsible = irresponsible*

If a word starts with *l*, you may use **il-**: *literate = illiterate*

1 Add the correct prefix to each word: *in-, im-, ir-, il-*, or *un-*.

1 ___appropriate	5 ___dependent	9 ___legal	13 ___practical
2 ___certain	6 ___experienced	10 ___mature	14 ___precise
3 ___conscious	7 ___fortunate	11 ___necessary	15 ___sufficient
4 ___convenient	8 ___intelligent	12 ___perfect	16 ___resistible

2 Complete the sentences. Use the words in the box and add a prefix when necessary.

appropriate	believable	dependent	inhabited
intelligent	popular	resistible	usual

In many parts of the world, a reality TV show called *Survivor* is extremely (1)_____. In the show, contestants compete in order to win a large cash prize. Contestants are taken to a remote, (2)_____ island. There, they are divided into two teams. Contestants are only given a large knife, a pot, and a water bottle for survival. The teams face a different challenge each week, and TV viewers are usually amazed and shocked by the (3)_____ things the contestants must do to survive. Sometimes the challenge is to solve an (4)_____ puzzle by using brain power and teamwork. Contestants must be very athletic, (5)_____, (6)_____, and have a strong personality. Often there are very sharp conflicts between the teams, and contestants make many (7)_____ comments. Of course, the personal drama is what makes the show (8)_____ to TV viewers. Each week, one or two contestants are removed from the island. In the end, there is only one survivor, who wins the grand prize.

WRITING Describing a challenging situation

You are going to learn about describing cause and effect and using the unreal conditional in the past. You are then going to use these skills to write two or three paragraphs to describe a situation in the past where you were in some sort of danger.

Writing skill

WRITING ABOUT CAUSE AND EFFECT

Useful words and phrases because, since, as, owing to X because of X Y is the result of … X (an) effect of … is (a) consequence of … is therefore, as a result	**Owing to** the mental confusion, a person doesn't realize what is happening. **As a consequence of** the mental confusion, a person doesn't realize what is happening. There is some mental confusion. **Therefore** a person doesn't realize what is happening.
Verbs make, cause, produce, generate, create, enable, lead to	One of the early symptoms of hypothermia is the inability to think clearly, which leads to a person **making** bad decisions/which **makes** a person **make** bad decisions/ which **causes** a person **to make** bad decisions.

1 In each pair of phrases, write *C* (cause) and *E* (effect).

1. ___ lack of insulation / ___ loss of body heat
2. ___ knew how to stay warm in snowstorm / ___ took a survival course
3. ___ eating high-energy food / ___ the body can generate energy
4. ___ suffering early hypothermia / ___ the person becomes confused
5. ___ dressed him in warm, dry clothing / ___ felt extremely cold
6. ___ sweating / ___ skin feels wet and cold

2 Cross out the word or phrase which **cannot** be used in each sentence.

1. A sweatshirt will not keep you warm. **Owing to / Because of / A result of** its lack of insulation, you will experience a loss of body heat.
2. The campers had taken a survival course. **As a consequence of / As a result / Therefore** they knew how to stay warm.
3. Sweating **produces / enables / generates** moisture. The moisture **makes the skin feel / causes the skin to feel / creates the skin to feel** wet and cold.
4. Eating high-energy foods **enables / allows / produces** the body to generate energy needed to stay warm.
5. **Since / Because of / As** the boy was wet and felt extremely cold, we quickly dressed him in warm, dry clothing.
6. **A consequence / A result / Therefore** of sweating is that the skin can become wet and cold.

3 **Discuss the situations with a partner. Use the expressions in parentheses to express cause and effect.**

1 As a result of walking in the hot sun, I got very dehydrated. (make)
2 I got lost in the mountains because of the fog. (As a consequence)
3 If people don't get enough sleep they can't drive safely. (cause)
4 Thanks to wearing fluorescent clothing, the lifeboat crew saw us very easily. (therefore)
5 Using the glow from my cell phone, I was able to find my way through the cave. (enable)

Grammar

UNREAL CONDITIONAL IN THE PAST

We can use the unreal conditional to talk about what could have happened in the past (but didn't).

Form	Example
If + *had* + past participle + modal verb + *have* + past participle	*If Callahan had had a sail, his time at sea would have been much shorter.*
The *if* clause can also come second	*He could have sailed the raft to Cape Verde if he'd had a sail.*
Use *might* to express a possible result	*Callahan might not have survived if he hadn't been so inventive.*

1 **Complete the sentences about Steven Callahan.**

1 If the boat _____ (not sink) so quickly, he _____ (be) able to get more supplies off the boat.

2 If Callahan _____ (not know) so much about the sea and navigation, he _____ (not estimate) his location and progress.

3 He _____ (lose) his muscle strength if he _____ (not exercise) daily.

4 He _____ (die) of thirst if he _____ (not devise) a 'still' for collecting water.

5 If he _____ (not have) the know-how to repair his fishing spear, he _____ (not have) anything to eat.

6 If he _____ (maintain) his positive attitude, he _____ (give up) hope about being found alive.

2 **Read each sentence. Write another sentence using the unreal conditional in the past to tell what would/might have happened differently. Compare your sentences with a partner.**

1 The driver almost hit me when I crossed the street.
2 I didn't do very well on my last test.
3 My essay was good, except that I included some irrelevant details.
4 When my uncle fell in the living room, he started a chain reaction of events, resulting in a broken chair, a broken lamp, and a broken wrist.
5 Yesterday there was a light breeze on the lake, so it was a perfect day for my first sailing lesson.

WRITING TASK

Write three paragraphs about a challenging situation in the past. You can write about a true situation or an imaginary one.

Audience: classmates/peers
Context: school newspaper
Purpose: to describe a dangerous situation

BRAINSTORM

1 Read the paragraph which gives advice on precautions to take when driving. Find and <u>underline</u> the thesis statement and two cause-effect statements.

After surviving my own treacherous driving experience in the desert, I've learned that driving across the desert in hot weather requires careful planning and preparation. First it is important to have plenty of gas. Because you will be using your air conditioner to cool the interior of the car, you will be using more gas. It's also essential to have plenty of coolant in your car in order to cool the engine. Safety experts recommend that you start with a full tank of gas and carry extra water and coolant for your car. In addition, you should have several liters of water to drink and food that will not spoil in the heat. You will need to drink more water than usual due to the extreme heat. Of course, a good map, a well-charged cell phone, and a first aid kit are also necessary. The next time you plan a trip during hot weather, take a tip from me: be prepared.

2 Think of a situation to write about using one of the ideas below or your own idea. List the details of what happened on a time line. Then in a small group, describe the situation and answer any questions classmates have about what happened. Talk about causes and effects.

- driving in the desert
- driving in the winter
- traveling in an unsafe area
- scuba diving

PLAN

Make an outline for each of the following paragraphs.

Paragraph 1: Describe the dangerous situation and what happened. Include as many details as possible. You can include mention of some causes and effects.

Paragraph 2: Describe what might have happened differently and how the dangerous situation could have been avoided. You should be able to use the unreal conditional in the past.

Paragraph 3: Conclude with recommendations about precautions to take to be safe and what you should have with you. Use passive modals to give advice (see Unit 6, page 64).

In your outline, include supporting details and examples. Check your outline against the assignment details for each paragraph. Have you included the required information?

WRITE

Write a three-paragraph narrative. When you finish, check that you have followed the instructions for each paragraph. Include new vocabulary from the unit, if possible.

SHARE

Exchange papers with a partner. Read the checklist on page 109 and provide feedback to your partner.

REWRITE AND EDIT

Consider your partner's comments and write a final draft of your essay.

Using desired outcomes to guide study strategy

by Stella Cottrell

Your reasons for studying and your desired outcomes can guide the way you proceed with your study, as in the following examples.

Outcome A: to learn about the subject

If learning about the subject is the most important outcome for you, then reading around the subject and doing what interests you may be more important than following the curriculum.

Outcome B: to have a good grade

If your main priority is getting a good grade, then it is likely to be important that you 'play the game' and find out exactly what is required.

Outcome C: just to get through

If you have many other demands on your time, or gaps in your education, you may have to limit yourself to covering essentials. What is important is that you know how to find and use information to get you through — you can fill gaps in your knowledge later in life.

Stating your desired outcomes

Outcomes are most motivating when stated in the present:

I am able to achieve a 2.1!

It is also best to state them as positive objectives:

I am able to gain a good job.

(Negatively formed outcomes, such as 'A degree will help me to escape from my current employment', are less effective in providing motivation.)

The effect of thinking negatively

Having a negative outcome is like going shopping with a list of what you are not going to buy.

O'Connor and McDermott (1996)

Analyze desired outcomes in detail

The following questions are based on an approach known as Neuro-Linguistic Programming (NLP).

Are your desired outcomes 'well-formed'?

- Are the desired outcomes clear and specific?
- Are they at all limiting?
- Do they help you?
- Are they realistic?
- Are they sufficiently motivating?
- Are the outcomes worth it?
- Are they really desirable?
- How will you know you have achieved the outcomes — what will be different?

What are the implications of having these desired outcomes?

- Will you need to put everything else on hold?
- Will you have to change your study options?
- Who else will be affected?
- Are there other implications?

What are the potential gains?

- Will you feel more in control of your life?
- Will you have more respect for yourself?
- Are there other potential gains?

What are the potential losses?

- Will you see less of family and friends?
- What sacrifices are involved?
- Are there other potential losses?

Visualize yourself in the future, having achieved the outcome

- Where are you as a result of your achievement?
- Are there any good or bad consequences?
- What has changed for you?
- Are you as happy as you thought you would be?

Drive

READING	Identifying important details
	Identifying sources of information
VOCABULARY	Idioms related to success
WRITING	Effective hooks
GRAMMAR	Intensifier + comparative combinations

Discussion point

Discuss these quotes and sayings with a partner. Explain their meanings in your own words. Do you agree with the quotations? Why or why not?

'The man who can drive himself further once the effort gets painful is the man who will win.'
Roger Bannister

'Everybody is born with an equal chance to become just as unequal as he or she possibly can.'
Anonymous

Vocabulary preview

Read the sentences. Then (circle) the word or phrase that is closest in meaning to the bold words.

1 Climbing Mount Everest was the greatest **achievement** of his life.
   a success   b fear

2 Julio's **ambition** is to become mayor of his city someday.
   a job   b goal

3 This team has the skill and **determination** to win the championship.
   a sense of humor   b strength of mind

4 If this **drought** continues, many farmers may go out of business.
   a cold weather   b dry weather

5 Top athletes must **endure** many hours of difficult training in all conditions.
   a continue through   b watch over

6 The desire to be accepted by our peers is **inherent** in all humans.
   a natural   b unusual

7 Janek has written **numerous** job applications, but so far without success.
   a a few   b many

8 A large **proportion** of high school students feel some stress about the future.
   a size   b percentage

READING 1 Making a difference

Before you read

Work with a partner. Think of an experience when you worked hard to achieve something. What was it? What helped you achieve it?

Global reading

Look at the questions about William Kamkwamba. Then read *Making a difference* and make notes on the answers.

1 What was William's life like when he was growing up?
2 Describe what education he has had.
3 What helped him achieve his goal?
4 What are some of his other achievements?

Close reading

IDENTIFYING IMPORTANT DETAILS

Determining your reasons for reading a text will help you decide which information is important. Follow these tips to help you identify important details in a text:

- Before you read, ask yourself, *What do I want to know about this topic? What do I need to know?*

- When reading an academic text for a class, read any discussion questions first, so you can focus on information you will need to talk about.

- When taking a test that involves a reading text, read all of the questions and answer choices first.

- Use your skills for scanning and reading fluently to find information quickly.

Read the statements. Then read *Making a difference* again and complete the statements.

1 As a young boy, William was expected to _____

2 Most people in rural Malawi go to bed early because _____

3 In the year 2000, Malawi _____

4 William got the idea to build a windmill from _____

5 At age 14, William _____

6 Today, William's village _____

ACADEMIC KEYWORDS

accept	(v)	/ək'sept/
material	(n)	/mə'tɪriəl/
reality	(n)	/ri'æləti/

Making a
difference

[1] Growing up in rural Malawi, Africa, William Kamkwamba learned to accept that life was hard. He lived with his parents and seven sisters in a small clay house without electricity or running water. Like most boys in his village, William was expected to assist his parents on the family farm, as well as keep up with his school work. Each night, like most Malawians, his family went to bed early because the kerosene oil they needed to light the lamps was costly.

[2] A terrible drought in 2000 left many Malawians hungry, and William's family was no exception. In 2003, at the age of 13, William and many other children were forced to drop out of school when their parents could no longer afford the tuition. William had to work <u>even harder</u> to help his family, but he wasn't ready to give up his education. He went to the local library and took out some books to study. One book, called *Using Energy*, sparked William's interest in science and gave him an idea that significantly changed his future.

[3] In the book, William found a picture of a windmill, and a brief description of how it could be used to generate electricity from wind. He knew that there was plenty of wind in his village, and realized that if he could build a windmill like that, he could give his family and the people in his village a <u>much better</u> life.' There was just one problem. The book didn't explain how to build a windmill, and neither did any of the other books in the library.

[4] What happened over the next year demonstrated William's incredible ambition and determination. He began to collect any kinds of materials he thought could be useful—scraps of wood, broken bicycles, old shoes—and started to build a windmill next to his family's house. He endured many challenges and failures. Other people in his village called him crazy and said his idea would never work. Finally, at the age of 14, William completed his first windmill. When they

saw electric lights and heard the sound of music on the radio coming from William's house, the village people came running. He had done it. William Kamkwamba had found a way to capture the wind.

[5] Kamkwamba's autobiography, *The Boy Who Harnessed the Wind*, tells the story of how the rest of the world came to know about his achievements. With the help of international supporters, his village now has clean running water, solar powered lighting, and electric power. As a result of his actions, Kamkwamba was invited to study engineering at Dartmouth College, one of the top-ranking universities in the U.S. He also travels the world and gives talks about how he made his dream a reality.

Developing critical thinking

Discuss these questions in a group.

1 Describe your reaction to William's story. How do you think the attitudes of the people in his village changed after his success?

2 What words would you use to describe William's personality? Do you (or does someone you know) share any of the same traits? Which ones?

READING 2 Most likely to succeed

Before you read

What do you think makes a person successful? Work in groups to write a definition of success.

THINK ABOUT:

achievement   career
fame   money
power   relationships

Global reading

IDENTIFYING SOURCES OF INFORMATION

In academic texts, writers often cite sources to support the information they are presenting. Especially when doing your own research, it's useful to identify these sources, so that you can refer to them for more information, if you so choose. These might include:

- interviews – quotations from experts in a particular field
- scholarly journals – publications in a specific field, such as psychology or medicine; articles written by researchers presenting the findings of their research studies
- popular journals – magazines intended to reach a wide audience; include articles on a variety of topics
- almanacs – facts and statistics about a particular topic, usually updated annually
- encyclopedia – a collection of facts about many different topics
- websites – information may include any of the above.

Additionally, because so much information is available online, it is important to compare information from various sources to ensure its accuracy and reliability.

Read *Most likely to succeed*. Underline the places where the writer cites a specific source. Then write your answers to these questions.

1 What types of sources are used in the article?
2 What information does each source give?
3 Where might you look if you wanted to consult those same sources to continue your own research?

ACADEMIC KEYWORDS

balance	(n)	/ˈbæləns/
combination	(n)	/ˌkɑmbɪˈneɪʃ(ə)n/
inherent	(adj)	/ɪnˈhɪrənt/

Close reading

Read *Most likely to succeed* again. Circle the correct information.

1 In order to achieve success, people need determination, energy, and **money / goals**.
2 One thing that high-achievers have in common is that they **are persistent / have high brain function**.
3 Parents can help their kids be confident if they **teach them ambition / accept their failures**.
4 People from middle-class backgrounds are more likely to be successful because they **don't have too much anxiety / have financial stress**.
5 Some high school students are **quitting their after-school jobs / doing more activities outside of school**.
6 An idea for relieving pressure to succeed is to **appreciate our friends and family / better our lives at any cost**.

MOST LIKELY TO SUCCEED

[1] **When it comes to ambition,** no two people are alike. Every class has its straight-A students, every company its go-getters, and every family its overachievers. Yet, for every one of these success-hunters, there's someone else who's perfectly satisfied with whatever life brings. What is it that sets us apart? What drives some people to study late into the night, work 80 hours a week, or practice a piano concerto until their fingers ache?

[2] Researchers say it's a combination of factors that determine a person's desire to achieve. Psychologist Larry Nas, from Northfork University, says, 'It's important to have drive. But we won't get anywhere if we don't know how to set clear goals.' Nas says that people may have goals, but without the ambition to get started, they end up simply talking about their plans for greatness, but never taking the first steps to achieve them. Similarly, those with inherent ambition and drive but no clear goals tend to begin numerous projects, but don't ever follow them to completion. In other words, without the right combination of personal characteristics and clear goals, we just spin our wheels.

[3] It's unclear whether ambition is guided more by genetics, or by outside factors like economic status and education, but psychologists believe that the trait is both genetic and learned. A recent study published in the Worthington University Journal measured *persistence* — the ability to stay focused on a task until it has been completed properly. In the study, researchers asked students to perform tasks, such as sorting photos. Those students who were the most persistent — those who felt strongly about completing the task and performing it well — had a significantly higher level of activity in the same area of the brain: the part which controls emotions. Despite these results, it's clear that persistence is more than just a brain function; it's also a learned habit.

[4] There aren't any strict rules about how to 'teach' ambition or about the outside factors that influence it. However, many high achievers do share some things in common. Most psychologists agree that it helps to have parents who encourage us to try new challenges, and who praise our successes and accept our failures. Jane West of the popular parenting website, best4kidz.net, says these types of home environments produce kids with much higher confidence levels, who learn how to set goals, work hard for them, and keep trying until they achieve them.

[5] In addition, economics plays an interesting role. In developed societies, a large proportion of successful people come from middle class backgrounds. According to an article in the December issue of *Hour Magazine*, the reason for this is what's known as 'status anxiety'. Middle-classers tend to have the right level of financial stress — a little, but not so much that they feel hopeless. This bit of stress actually helps drive middle classers to improve their status and work extra hard to avoid falling down the socio-economic ladder.

Unfortunately, the drive for success can create its own stress. Sixteen-hour work days, fast food meals, and pressure to out-perform colleagues can lead to stress-related illnesses, such as sleep problems, stomach pain, and heart attacks. These days, even teens and young adults are feeling the pressure. Competition to get into good colleges and eventually find good jobs has high school students pushing themselves harder than ever. The Owen State University website recently published the results of its survey of 600 high school students at a top-ranking high school. Most of the kids reported feeling pressure to take advanced-level courses, participate in sports or clubs, and do after-school jobs. Not surprisingly, about 70% of those surveyed reported that they felt stress some or all of the time.

[6] So, on which side of the fence is the grass really greener? Is it better to get out of the rat race and avoid all that unhealthy stress? Or should we continue the quest to better ourselves and our lives at any cost? For many, it's difficult to find the balance. One trick may be to remember to appreciate our non-material wealth — family, friendship, and doing the things we enjoy. Most would agree that those treasures are far more valuable than any material wealth or success.

Developing critical thinking

1 Discuss these questions in a group.

1 The article claims that while there are some people who are driven to be high achievers, others are 'perfectly happy with whatever life brings.' Which type of person are you most similar to? Why do you think so? What do you think might have made you the way you are?

2 Do you agree with the writer's suggestion at the end of the article for how to find the balance between stress and success? What other suggestions help people avoid feeling the pressure to succeed?

2 Think about the ideas from *Making a difference* and *Most likely to succeed* and discuss these questions in a group.

1 Who is the most successful person you know? How did they achieve their success?

2 Tell your partner about an idea you have that you have not yet followed through. What stopped you?

Vocabulary skill

IDIOMS RELATED TO SUCCESS

The meaning of idioms can sometimes be difficult to guess. Therefore, it is helpful to study and learn them as set phrases. When you read or hear idioms, write them down in a notebook. Then look them up later in a dictionary or online. Here are some examples from *Making a difference*:

go-getter	*The grass is always greener on the other side.*
straight-A student	*(to get out of / join) the rat race*
at any cost	*(to climb / fall down) the social ladder*

1 Find the expressions from the skill box in *Making a difference* on page 81. Use the context to help you determine their meaning. Then match them with definitions below.

a someone who always gets top grades
b ambitious person
c life seems better somewhere else
d situation where everyone is too busy to enjoy themselves
e however difficult it is
f levels you move up or down in society

2 Complete these sentences using the correct form of an expression from the skill box.

1 Carla invited all of her co-workers to her birthday party. She is trying to _____ at work.

2 Last year, Jo was a _____, but her grades are slipping this year.

3 She's a real _____. I think she'll make it to the top!

4 Things are too competitive at work. I want to get out of _____.

5 You want Ken's life? Have you ever heard the saying, '_____'? It means other people's lives always seem better than your own.

6 I can see you're going to get that promotion _____, even if you have to work every evening and every weekend! You'll go far!

3 Work with a partner. Find two more idioms related to success in exercise 2 and discuss what you think they mean.

WRITING A proposal

You are going to learn about using effective hooks and practice making intensifier and comparative combinations. You are then going to use these to make a plan for a business or project that will have a positive effect on your school, neighborhood, town, or city.

Writing skill

EFFECTIVE HOOKS

A hook is a useful writing technique used to grab the reader's interest. It is usually at the very beginning of the introduction. Read the following hooks for a business proposal to build a new playground:

A strong statement	*The children of Homeville have waited far too long for a playground.*
A question	*Do you believe it's important for children to play outdoors in the fresh air?*
An anecdote	*Rina is a first grader at Homeville Elementary School. Like most children, she loves to run, jump and climb. The problem, she says, is that downtown Homeville has no place for smaller children to play outside after school and on weekends.*
A statistic	*Studies show that 60% of children under the age of 10 do not spend enough time outdoors or get the recommended amount of exercise.*

1 **Read the paragraph and add a hook. Choose from one of the types in the skill box.**

_____. The building on the corner of Cherry and Green Streets would be a perfect location for our frozen yogurt shop. This business would give residents a much healthier alternative to the fast food, candy, and ice cream shops currently available downtown.

2 **Work in a group. Choose four of the following business or project ideas. On a separate piece of paper, write a hook to begin a proposal for each business or project. Use a different type of hook for each one.**

- a childcare center
- a concert hall / theater
- a computer repair shop
- a garden
- a health club
- an ice cream shop
- a recycling center
- a senior center
- a skateboard park
- a swimming pool

3 **Share your hooks with the class.**

Grammar

INTENSIFIER + COMPARATIVE COMBINATIONS

Intensifiers are words and phrases that add emphasis or express varying degrees. For example:

a bit	much	a great deal
a little	far	a lot
slightly	even	significantly

You can add intensifiers to comparative adjectives in order to express a degree of comparison.

*The new ice cream shop will be **even busier** in the summer.*

*Building costs will be **a great deal higher** next year, so we should act now.*

They can also be used in academic writing for hedging.

1 Find the four <u>underlined</u> examples of intensifier + comparatives in *Making a difference* and *Most likely to succeed*.

2 You are going to create a proposal for one of the businesses or projects in Writing skill exercise 2. Complete the sentences using intensifiers and the comparative adjectives from the box. Write sentences to include in a business proposal.

Intensifiers			Adjectives
a bit	much	a great deal	safer / more dangerous
a little	far	a lot	cleaner / dirtier
slightly	even	significantly	busier / quieter
			smaller / larger
			more costly / less expensive
			more enjoyable / less boring
			more modern / less old-fashioned

1 A new recycling center _____.

2 Building a concert hall _____.

3 The city's parks _____.

4 The senior center _____.

5 Exercising in a health club _____.

6 A computer repair shop _____.

7 The new skateboard park _____.

8 Our school campus _____.

WRITING TASK

Write a proposal for a business or a project that will improve people's lives in your community.

Audience: classmates/peers
Context: business / project proposal
Purpose: to describe how a project will improve peoples' lives

BRAINSTORM

Think of a business or a project (e.g. park, community center) that would improve the lives of people at your school, or in your neighborhood, town, or city. You can use your own idea or choose one of the ideas from Writing Exercise 2 on page 83. List the ways this business would improve people's lives.

PLAN

Discuss the questions and write answers.

1 What problems will the new business or project help?
2 Who will it benefit?
3 What will be the positive results?
4 When will the project begin? How long will it take?
5 What does your team need to complete the job (e.g. money, staff)?

WRITE

1 Write a hook for your proposal on a separate piece of paper. Choose one of the types on page 83.
2 Write a one-page proposal. Explain your plan and its benefits in detail. Use intensifiers and comparative adjectives where possible. Follow this outline.

- Paragraph 1: Include a hook that explains the problem. Give a brief introduction to the plan and who/what it will help.
- Paragraph 2: List the positive effects the project/business will have. Give examples and details to support your claims.
- Paragraph 3: Explain when the project will take place and where. Give an estimate for how long it will take from start to finish.
- Explain in detail your needs for the project. How much will it cost? How many staff do you need? What additional considerations are there? Give reasons to support your requests.

SHARE

Exchange papers with a partner. Does the proposal follow the outline above? Is there a hook in the introduction? Which type is it? Does it grab the reader's attention?

REWRITE AND EDIT

Consider your partner's comments and rewrite your proposal.

STUDY SKILLS Selecting and evaluating online sources

Getting started

Discuss these questions with a partner.

1 How many times a week do you use the Internet for these activities?
   - to get the news
   - to find out about historical events
   - to do research for a school paper or project
   - to get ideas for places to go on vacation
   - to get driving directions
2 Have you ever found information that was incorrect or untrue on the Internet? How did you find out? What was the result?
3 Why do you think it is important to check the reliability of information you find on the Internet?

Scenario

Read the scenario and think about what Mariana is doing right and what she is doing wrong.

Consider it

Look at these tips for evaluating online sources. Which ones do you already follow? Which ones are most useful to you?

1 **Determine your needs** Before you start researching, ask yourself what sources or what kinds of sources will be most likely to provide the information you need.
2 **Go straight to the experts** Select reliable sources that specialize in your topic. For example, for academic topics, use university websites, metropolitan newspapers, academic journals, hospital websites, etc. For most academic writing, using an online encyclopedia is not acceptable.
3 **Check for credibility** Look for information that indicates that the site or article is reliable, for example, the author's education and training, contact information, references to respected organizations, citations, and a bibliography of references.
4 **Make sure information is current** Look for dates on documents and web sites to make sure they include information that is updated regularly.
5 **Check facts and figures on multiple sources** Any facts, numerical statistics, or claims should be checked for accuracy on two or three websites.
6 **Keep good records** In addition to bookmarking any websites you use, write down or copy and paste the url (the complete web address) and the date you accessed it onto a document, in case a website is no longer accessible later.

Over to you

Discuss these questions with a partner.

1 What are the potential problems with not evaluating Internet sources before using them for research?
2 What are some other things that are important to keep in mind when using the Internet for academic research?
3 The next time you use the Internet for research purposes, what might you do differently? Which tips above will you try?

Like most university students, Mariana usually uses the Internet to do research for class assignments and projects. Depending on her topic of research, she types key search words or a question into her web browser to find a list of possible sources. She clicks on the first link at the top of the list and begins reading it and taking notes for her report. She keeps a list of the links she uses, and she also adds a 'bookmark' on her computer for each one. When she needs more information, she continues searching other sites, taking notes, and bookmarking/listing the links she uses until she has a very long list of many sources. When she is doing research for a persuasive essay, she is careful to consult sites that show both sides of people's opinions.

Sound

READING	Identifying tone and mood
VOCABULARY	Descriptive adjectives
WRITING	Using similes and metaphors
GRAMMAR	Cleft sentences with *what*

Discussion point

Discuss these questions with a partner.

1 How loud do you imagine the sound of a waterfall might be?
   What could you compare it to? How far away do you think it could be heard?

2 Look at the phrases that describe sounds. Rank the phrases, going from
   the softest (1) to the loudest (10).

___ bang of a drum   ___ bark of a dog
___ crash of a glass breaking   ___ honk of a car horn
___ whisper of a child   ___ screech of brakes on a train
___ hum of a clothes dryer   ___ scratch of a pencil across the page
___ buzz of a bee   ___ boom of thunder

Vocabulary preview

Complete the paragraph with the correct form of the words in the box.

| affect | audible | cease | confuse | distinguish | roar | sweep | trouble |

I recently had an ear infection, and it greatly (1) _____ my hearing. I couldn't (2) _____ between my friends' voices in a conversation. Their words were barely (3) _____. In frustration, I (4) _____ listening, and just read a magazine. Later, at the train station, I could scarcely hear the (5) _____ of the approaching train and so, was (6) _____ when it seemed to suddenly appear. When the doors of the train opened, the crowd of people (7) _____ me into the car. I was so (8) _____ by that experience and the growing pain in my ear that I went directly to the doctor.

READING 1 *The Secret Garden*: An excerpt

Before you read

Write answers to the question. Then discuss it with a partner.

When you were young, do you remember a place that was secret or mysterious or where you used to hide? Where was it? What did you do there? Did you play games, read, talk with a friend?

Global reading

1 Read the excerpt from *The Secret Garden*. Answer the questions.

1 Where are Mary and Martha in this part of the story?
2 Where does Mary think the crying sound is coming from?
3 What caused the door to blow open?
4 Martha has a different way of talking. How does the author show this?

The Secret Garden: An excerpt

IDENTIFYING TONE AND MOOD

When you read, you will feel affected by the language the author uses and the images the author creates. In literature as well as in more factual kinds of writing, you will need to be aware of the **tone** of writing. Tone is the author's attitude toward the story or topic, or even the audience. The author's tone can be humorous, serious, understanding, or critical. The tone can also refer to informal or formal language.

The author also uses language to create a **mood** or feeling. Words can communicate feelings of happiness, sadness, or humor — almost any emotion you can name. In a story, the mood changes, depending on what is happening. Noticing the mood can help you understand the story. Authors of non-fiction, however, do not use language to create mood.

2 Find a sentence in *The Secret Garden* which shows each mood in the box.

| mysterious | puzzled | scary | suspicious |

Close reading

Find and underline each of the words below in *The Secret Garden*. Read the context around the word. Then match the word to the definition.

Paragraph 2
1 shuddering ___   a cold air that blows into a room
2 buffeting ___   b hallway

Paragraph 4
3 wailing ___   c clearly

Paragraph 5
4 draught ___   d not willing to change your mind
5 passage ___   e keep hitting with force
6 plainly ___   f shaking

Paragraph 7
7 stubbornly ___   g crying

Frances Hodgson Burnett

¹ *In **'The Secret Garden'**, a novel written by Frances Hodgson Burnett in 1911, young Mary Lennox arrives from India to live with her uncle in Yorkshire, England. Her parents have died during an epidemic in India, and Mary is now alone. In India, she had grown up isolated from other children, and is an angry and lonely girl. At her uncle's house, she is often by herself and begins to explore the big quiet house. It seems to hold many mysteries and secrets. One night, she is sitting and talking with Martha, a young maid. Martha tells Mary to listen to the wind 'wutherin'' around the house.*

² Mary did not know what 'wutherin'' meant until she listened, and then she understood. It must mean that hollow, shuddering sort of roar which rushed round and round the house, as if the giant no one could see were buffeting it and beating at the walls and windows to try to break in. But one knew he could not get in, and somehow it made one feel very safe and warm inside a room with a red coal fire.

Sitting by the fire, Mary asks Martha questions about her uncle and the house. After a while, they fall silent, listening to the wind blowing outside and watching the fire.

³ But as she was listening to the wind she began to listen to something else. She did not know what it was, because at first she could scarcely distinguish it from the wind itself. It was a curious sound — it seemed almost as if a child were crying somewhere. Sometimes the wind sounded rather like a child crying, but presently Mistress Mary felt quite sure that this sound was inside the house, not outside it. It was far away, but it was inside. She turned round and looked at Martha.

⁴ 'Do you hear anyone crying?' she said.

Martha suddenly looked confused.

'No,' she answered. 'It's th' wind. Sometimes it sounds as if someone was lost on th' moor an' wailin'. It's got all sorts o' sounds.'

'But listen,' said Mary. 'It's in the house — down one of those long corridors.'

⁵ And at that very moment a door must have been opened somewhere downstairs; for a great rushing draught blew along the passage and the door of the room they sat in was blown open with a crash, and as they both jumped to their feet the light was blown out and the crying sound was swept down the far corridor, so that it was to be heard more plainly than ever.

⁶ 'There!' said Mary. 'I told you so! It is someone crying—and it isn't a grown-up person.' Martha ran and shut the door and turned the key, but before she did it they both heard the sound of a door in some far passage shutting with a bang, and then everything was quiet, for even the wind ceased 'wutherin'' for a few moments.

⁷ 'It was th' wind,' said Martha stubbornly. 'An' if it wasn't, it was little Betty Butterworth, th' scullery-maid. She's had th' toothache all day.' But something troubled and awkward in her manner made Mistress Mary stare very hard at her. She did not believe she was speaking the truth.

From: *The Secret Garden*, Frances Hodgson Burnett, London: Penguin Books Ltd., 1911.

Developing critical thinking

Discuss these questions in a group.

1 What could be making the crying sound? Give reasons.
2 What can you infer about daily life from the story?

ACADEMIC KEYWORDS

distinguish	(v)	/dɪˈstɪŋgwɪʃ/
far	(adj)	/fɑr/
some	(det)	/sʌm/

READING 2 The loudest sound you've never heard

Before you read

For academic reading, it is a good idea to quickly scan the text so that you can adjust your reading strategies to the task. Scan *The loudest sound you've never heard* on the next page and answer the questions. Then discuss your answers with a partner.

1 Look at the title and the box of science terms. What terms do you already know? Is this a familiar or unfamiliar topic for you?

2 What information does the photo give you about the topic?

3 How many paragraphs are in the article? How long will it take you to read the article?

Global reading

1 Read *The loudest sound you've never heard* and answer the questions.

  1 What is the tone of this article? Circle the word or words.
    academic   formal   humorous   informal

  2 This article does not have a mood. Why not?

2 Read the topic notes. Match the notes to the paragraph number. There are two extra topics that are not in the article. Mark those with an *X*.

___ *Infrasound – heard by animals.*	___ *Discovery of infrasound*
___ *Can be created by many natural events*	___ *Travels through earth and ocean; can be measured*
___ *How infrasound affects humans*	___ *Best methods for measuring sound frequencies*
___ *Can create health problems in humans*	___ *Infrasound – less than 20 hertz, very low*

Close reading

1 Read the sentences. Write *T* (True) or *F* (False) according to *The loudest sound you've never heard*. Then correct the false statements.

  1 Scientists cannot measure sounds that are less than 20 hertz. ___

  2 The Krakatoa Volcano erupted in Italy. ___

  3 Meteorologists can use data about infrasound to predict air turbulence. ___

  4 Before a volcano erupts, there is a great decrease in infrasound. ___

  5 Some birds use infrasound to navigate. ___

  6 Supersonic jets create infrasound. ___

  7 Experiments have shown that about 80% of people may be affected by infrasound. ___

2 Answer the questions.

  1 What is infrasound? Write a definition.

  2 How did infrasound from Krakotoa affect people?

  3 What natural events can create infrasound?

  4 How does infrasound change before a volcano erupts?

  5 Give an example of how an animal uses infrasound.

  6 How does infrasound affect humans?

ACADEMIC KEYWORDS		
associate	(v)	/əˈsoʊʃiˌeɪt/
increase	(n)	/ˈɪnˌkris/
predict	(v)	/prɪˈdɪkt/

The loudest
sound you've never heard

[1] What do elephants, whales, alligators, hurricanes, and manmade explosions all have in common? They all can create infrasound, a mysterious sound that humans cannot hear. Humans can only hear sounds within a certain range of frequency. The frequency (the number of cycles of vibration per second) of sound is measured in a unit called a hertz. Humans can hear sounds from 20 Hz (hertz) to 20kHz (20,000 hertz), but scientists are able to measure sounds at much lower hertz. Infrasound is less than 20 hertz, which is a frequency too low for humans to hear.

[2] Scientists first became aware of the existence of infrasound in 1883, when the gigantic explosion of the Krakatoa volcano in Indonesia resulted in windows breaking hundreds of miles away and barometric pressure readings going haywire around the world. Scientists realized that the volcano created a massive yet inaudible infrasound, sweeping through the air around the world.

[3] Modern scientists are now collecting large amounts of infrasound data from measuring stations around the world. They have discovered that infrasound can be created by explosions, ocean storms, hurricanes, auroras (northern lights), and air turbulence. As they learn more about the infrasound patterns associated with certain situations, scientists can use the information to predict storms, volcanoes, and other disturbances. For example, airplanes are often tossed up and down by clear air turbulence, invisible air pockets that are not associated with bad weather. If meteorologists can distinguish the infrasound of air turbulence, they can warn pilots to avoid the dangerous areas.

[4] Infrasound can also be measured as it travels through the earth and ocean. Scientists are now measuring the rumblings of earthquakes and the powerful roars of volcanoes before they can be heard by humans. For example, researchers placed special microphones near the opening of Antarctica's Erebus volcano.

Even though they could hear practically nothing on the earth's surface, the underground devices measured a great deal of infrasound. Before the 1998 eruption of the Sakurajima volcano in Japan, infrasound instruments recorded a sharp increase in the frequency and power of the infrasound. Geologists have learned that infrasound is better for predicting a volcano than seismographic activity.

[5] To some creatures in the animal world, infrasound is loud and clear. Elephants make infrasounds that can be heard by other elephants up to 10 kilometers away, and can be heard through the ground up to 32 kilometers away. Infrasound travels much further in water, allowing some types of whales to communicate with each other across thousands of miles. Some birds use infrasound to navigate, and rock doves have heard infrasound measured at .05 Hz, an extremely low frequency. Understanding infrasound and how animals use it can increase our knowledge about animal behavior, but it can also show how our actions can disrupt these important sounds. For example, infrasound from supersonic jets, ships, and wind turbines has been shown to disrupt other natural infrasounds, leading animals to become confused and disoriented.

[6] Even though we humans can't hear infrasound, there is some evidence that we are affected by it. In a 2003 experiment in the United Kingdom, 750 concertgoers listened to four separate musical pieces. Unknown to the attendees, some of the music pieces were accompanied by infrasound. After the concert, 22% of the concertgoers reported feeling troubled by uneasiness, chills, and nervousness during the infrasound sections of the concert. There are many stories of people being affected by infrasound, but most of these lack true scientific evidence. More research needs to be done to support claims that people are affected in predictable ways by infrasound.

barometric pressure: pressure exerted by the atmosphere as measured by a barometer

meteorologist: scientist who studies the weather

seismographic: relating to measurement of strength of an earthquake

air turbulence: rapid changes in wind speed and direction, and up and down wind currents

wind turbine: a modern windmill designed to convert wind energy into electrical energy

Developing critical thinking

1 **Discuss these questions in a group.**

1 Would it be advantageous for humans to be able to hear infrasound? Why or why not? Make a list of the pros and cons.

2 In our daily lives, we are surrounded by all sorts of sounds. What sounds are the most pleasant or relaxing? Do you enjoy being in complete silence?

THINK ABOUT:

communication	dangerous
concerts	upsetting
weather	warning signs

2 Think about the ideas from *The Secret Garden: An excerpt* and *The loudest sound you've never heard* and discuss these questions in a group.

1 In *The Secret Garden*, Mary seems to hear things that Martha doesn't. Do you think that there may be some people who can hear infrasound? Why or why not?

2 Imagine a story about a person with the unusual ability to hear infrasound. What special things might this person be able to do? What would some of the difficulties be?

Vocabulary skill

DESCRIPTIVE ADJECTIVES

Knowing a wide variety of descriptive adjectives will improve your reading comprehension and your writing. Some general adjectives are over-used, such as *nice, good, bad, hard, loud,* and *big*. Using more specific adjectives makes a sentence more interesting. Compare the examples.

This is a **nice** cup of coffee.   This is a **delicious** cup of coffee.

It's a very **big** tree.   It's a **gigantic** tree.

There are a wide variety of adjectives for the senses. For example, adjectives related to sight can describe color, size, shape, and quality.

1 Which adjectives do <u>not</u> belong in each group?

1 Cross out the two adjectives that are **not** usually used to describe <u>sound</u>.

deafening	juicy	mysterious	shrill
high	muffled	round	soft

2 Cross out the two adjectives that are **not** usually used to describe <u>sight</u>.

bright	glamorous	narrow	square
damp	golden	noisy	steep

3 Cross out the two adjectives that are **not** usually used to describe <u>smell</u>.

fragrant	red	spicy	sweaty
friendly	smoky	strong	sweet

4 Cross out the two adjectives that are **not** usually used to describe <u>taste</u>.

bitter	delicious	salty	dusty
dark	fresh	sour	sweet

5 Cross out the two adjectives that are **not** usually used to describe <u>touch</u>.

bumpy	green	rough	warm
delicious	icy	soft	wet

2 Complete the paragraph with adjectives from exercise 1.

With a (1) _____ scream, I woke myself up from the nightmare. Shocked and suddenly wide awake, I laid still and wondered where I was. The air was (2) _____ and (3) _____, and I shivered under the thin blankets. Coming under the curtains was the (4) _____ light of dawn. I realized that I was in my own (5) _____ bed. My breathing slowed down, and I felt calmer. Inhaling, I could smell a (6) _____ breakfast. I could hear the (7) _____ sounds of people talking in the kitchen.

WRITING A descriptive anecdote

You are going to learn about using similes, metaphors, and cleft sentences with *what*. You are then going to use these to write an anecdote including some description.

Writing skill

USING SIMILES AND METAPHORS

When you write a story, you can use similes and metaphors to make it more interesting. Generally similes and metaphors are not used in more formal writing.

In a simile, you say that two things are similar using *like* or *as*.

It sounds **as if** someone was lost on the moor.

Infrasound is **like** the sound of a gigantic rumble that you can't hear.

A blast of infrasound from a whale can be **as** powerful **as** being physically hit.

In a metaphor, you say that one thing *is* another thing. It is a stronger image than a simile.

That hollow, shuddering sort of **roar** rushed round and round the house.

As I walked into the party I was **hit** by **a wall** of sound.

The silence was **deafening**.

1 **Answer the questions about *The Secret Garden*.**

  1 As well as the metaphor in the skill box above, the author introduces another metaphor for the wind in paragraph 2 of the text. What does she say the wind is?

  2 In paragraph 3, the author uses a simile to say what the sound was like. What is the simile?

2 **Use your imagination to complete this paragraph, based on paragraph 5 of *The Secret Garden*.**

But as I was listening to (1) _____, I began to listen to something else. I did not know what it was, because at first I could scarcely distinguish it from (2) _____. It was a (3) _____ sound—it seemed almost as if (4) _____ . Sometimes the (5) _____ sounded like (6) _____ , but soon I felt quite sure that this sound was (7) _____ . It was (8) _____ , but it was (9) _____ .

3 **Write sentences using the simile or metaphor.**

  1 'like a lion'
  2 'like Einstein'
  3 'as loud as a freight train' 'is a freight train'
  4 'as strong as an ox' 'is an ox'
  5 'as quiet as a mouse'
  6 'is my lifeline'

Grammar

CLEFT SENTENCES WITH *WHAT*

In a cleft sentence with *what*, the word order is changed to give emphasis to what comes first in the sentence. A *what*-clause is often used to emphasize emotions such as *like, need, feel, think, want, dislike* and *prefer*.

Form	Example
[*What* + noun/pronoun + emotive verb] + verb *to be* + noun or noun clause	We need to distinguish between real and imagined sounds. → **What we need to do** is to distinguish between real and imagined sounds.
A *what*-clause with the auxiliary *do* is used to emphasize the event or action.	He left the door unlocked. → **What he did** was leave the door unlocked.
[*What* + subject + *do*] + verb *to be* + verb clause	I analyze all of the experiment data. → **What I do** is analyze all of the experiment data.

1 **Mark the cleft sentences with a C. Mark the regular sentences with a check (✓). In the cleft sentences, <u>underline</u> the *what* clause.**

  1 What he did was measure the low sound frequencies. ____

  2 I didn't hear what she said. ____

  3 What the children love is playing in the water. ____

  4 He can listen and identify what instrument is being played. ____

  5 'What is the problem?' I asked. ____

  6 What they do is conduct experiments with infrasound. ____

2 **Rewrite the sentences as cleft sentences to emphasize the action or the emotion.**

  1 They decided to soundproof the music studio.

  2 I need to interview people who work with deaf people for my project.

  3 They want to discuss solutions to the problems of noise pollution.

  4 I felt upset that he wasn't listening to what I said.

  5 She always asks for the quietest room in the hotel.

  6 I love the sound of waves crashing on the shore.

3 **Complete each cleft sentence with your own information. Then share with a partner.**

  1 What I enjoy doing on the weekends _____

  2 What I feared during the storm _____

  3 What I dislike _____

  4 What I did _____

  5 What we did to _____

  6 What _____ does _____

WRITING TASK

In this writing task, you will write the beginning of an anecdote, a short retelling of something that happened to you or someone you know. Think of an anecdote in which sound was important in some way.

Audience:	peers/classmates
Context:	an anecdote or letter
Purpose:	to describe something that happened in an interesting way

BRAINSTORM

1 With a partner, discuss the possible topics. Choose one for your writing.

- a scary or frightening experience
- a good surprise
- an outdoor adventure
- a funny experience
- an unexpected event on a trip
- a very loud sound

2 Fill in the graphic organizer with ideas about your anecdote. Then decide what information to include. You do not need to include descriptions related to all five senses, but you do need to include a description of sounds.

The story	The senses
who	sound
what	sight
where	touch
when	taste
why and how	smell

PLAN

1 Briefly, tell your anecdote to your partner. Answer any questions. This will help you organize your anecdote and decide what information and details to include.

2 To make your writing more interesting, think of a simile or metaphor to include. Write it several different ways, and then choose the best version.

WRITE

Write your anecdote, using descriptive adjectives. Use a variety of sentence types, including simple, compound and complex sentences, and a cleft sentence.

SHARE

Exchange anecdotes with a partner. Read the checklist on page 109 and provide feedback to your partner.

REWRITE AND EDIT

Consider your partner's comments and write a final draft of your anecdote.

STUDY SKILLS Using the thesaurus

Getting started

Discuss these questions with a partner.

1 What type of dictionary do you use? What information does it include?
2 Do you use a dictionary to help you when you are writing? How does it help you?
3 Have you ever used a thesaurus to find synonyms (or antonyms)? When? For what types of writing?

Scenario

Read the scenario and think about what Kumar is doing right and what he is doing wrong.

Consider it

Look at these tips for using a thesaurus. Which ones do you already follow? Which ones are most useful to you?

1 **Know the benefits** The average thesaurus contains over 100,000 synonyms for words. Using a thesaurus can help you build your vocabulary, avoid repetition in your writing, express your ideas more accurately, and make your descriptions richer and more interesting.

2 **Know when to use it** Use a dictionary when you want to know the meaning of a particular word. Use a thesaurus when you already have a word in mind but feel that it does not express exactly what you want to say, when you want to avoid repeating a word in a passage, or when you are looking for a more (or less) formal/poetic/scientific, etc. word.

3 **Choose the right type** There are two types of thesaurus: those for general use are organized alphabetically, like a dictionary; the other type organizes words by theme or topic (e.g. medicine, music).

4 **Learn the features** In addition to synonyms, a thesaurus may list antonyms or contain topical word lists or other useful features.

5 **Be aware that synonyms aren't exact translations** No two words have exactly the same meaning nor convey the same tone, feeling, or level of formality. When in doubt, use the dictionary to double check meaning to help you make a choice for which word to choose.

6 **Check out electronic and online options** These days, many electronic dictionaries have thesaurus features. Smartphones have downloadable thesaurus apps, and there are many thesaurus websites. Choose the option that works best for you.

Over to you

Discuss these questions with a partner.

1 Which type of thesaurus would be most convenient and useful for you (e.g. printed book, electronic, online, alphabetical, topical)? Why?
2 What are the potential disadvantages of using a thesaurus?
3 What additional features would you ideally like to have in your thesaurus (e.g. antonyms, word lists, pronunciation information)? Why?

Kumar enjoys writing in English, and he even keeps an English journal, which he uses as a diary and for writing short stories and poems. This semester, he is taking a creative writing course for English majors. Sometimes he finds it hard to express his ideas because he isn't sure of the right vocabulary in English. He sometimes uses the dictionary when he wants to know the English translation for a word in his own language, but he finds it annoying to have to stop his writing often and check a big, bulky book. In these cases, he just uses simple words he already knows in English that have a similar meaning to the word in his first language. Two consistent comments from Kumar's writing teacher are that he should try to use more descriptive language in his writing and he needs to avoid repetition of the same words.

Tomorrow

READING	Recognizing the writer's attitude and bias
	Reading statistical data
VOCABULARY	Vocabulary for describing trends
WRITING	Qualifying statistical data
GRAMMAR	The future progressive

Discussion point

Discuss these questions with a partner.

1 Think about these topics. Twenty years from now, do you think they will be better or worse than they are now? Make one prediction for each one. Then share them with the class.

- communication
- the economy
- education
- employment
- the environment
- housing
- technology
- transportation

2 Choose one topic from question 1 that you think is important. What steps might people living today take in order to avoid problems and improve the situation in the future?

Vocabulary preview

Read the sentences. Circle the word that matches the word in bold in each sentence.

1 **Against** his parents' advice, Karl decided not to go to college immediately after high school.
   a Contrary to   **b** In contrast to   **c** Complimentary to

2 For many people, the **idea** of the Internet seemed unbelievable at first.
   a notion   **b** notification   **c** notary

3 Business owners will need to develop **plans** for achieving success in order to succeed.
   a statistics   **b** strategies   **c** states

4 Experts **state firmly** that weather patterns will continue to become more unpredictable in the future.
   a assault   **b** asset   **c** assert

5 Travel industry experts predict another **sudden increase** in airline prices this summer.
   a surge   **b** spill   **c** strike

6 The number of students who own tablet computers increased **twice as much** last year and is likely to double again this year.
   a twofold   **b** triple   **c** multiple

READING 1 Global graduates

Before you read

Look at the chart. What is the global trend in university education? Which countries show the greatest shifts?

Global reading

Read _Global graduates_. Then complete the sentences.

1 The article discusses trends in _____
2 According to the article, there has been an increase _____
3 Countries around the world _____
4 The goals of these countries include _____
5 A possible result of these trends _____

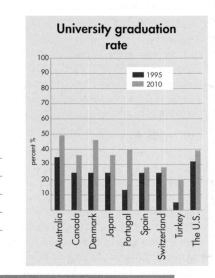

University graduation rate
■ 1995
■ 2010

Close reading

RECOGNIZING THE WRITER'S ATTITUDE AND BIAS

Writers often use a variety of language to express a range of feelings, such as humor, sarcasm, approval, or disagreement. When you read, look for words and phrases that express an opinion or a judgment.

Opinion adjectives: _astounding, attractive, better, best, shocking, wonderful, overrated, undervalued, worst_

Opinion adverbs and stance markers: _As expected, Most importantly, Not surprisingly, Interestingly, Undoubtedly, Perhaps, Most certainly_

Emotive verbs: _dislike, enjoy, hope, hate, love, prefer_

Read _Global graduates_ again. Decide if the sentences are (_T_) true or (_F_) false, according to the writer.

1 The overall tone of the article is critical.   ____
2 It's surprising that China has the largest university system in the world.   ____
3 A college degree is necessary to succeed in the current economy.   ____
4 The number of international universities in Qatar's Education City is impressive.   ____
5 Students were better off in the past.   ____

GLOBAL GRADUATES

▪ INTERNATIONAL GRADS ON THE RISE

[1] *Scientia potentia est* is a Latin saying that means 'Knowledge is power'. According to some recent positive trends in education, young people around the world are taking the adage to heart. Over the past two decades, there has been a surge in the numbers of university graduates, as well as in the numbers of students studying internationally. The Organisation for Economic Co-operation and Development (OECD) reports that among a number of its developed member-nations, graduation rates have increased nearly two-fold since the mid-1990s (Education: crisis reinforces importance of a good education, 2011). Some countries are actively making an effort to encourage students to study abroad. Saudi Arabia, for example, started the King Abdullah Scholarship Program in 2005. The program pays for Saudi students to travel overseas to attend university.

[2] As expected, China leads the pack with the largest university system in the world. According to Chinese Education Ministry figures, close to a million students per year graduate from its 2,500+ institutions of higher education. Some experts assert that by 2020, there will be an astounding 35.5 million students enrolled in Chinese colleges and universities, many of them from nations other than China.

[3] Other countries from France to Oman to South Korea are also expanding their university systems to accommodate this swelling tide. With the global economic crisis resulting in fewer job opportunities and more competition for existing jobs, it's clear a college education — and better still, an international one — is becoming more a necessity than a luxury.

▪ GLOBAL KNOWLEDGE CENTERS

[4] Not only are individuals recognizing the value of international education, entire countries are expanding their educational offerings and developing strategies to attract the brightest and the best, and to sharpen their global competitive edge. In effect, says Philip Altbach, director of the Centre for International Higher Education, at Boston College, these nations are building a new type of economy: an economy of knowledge. (Graduates: the new measure of power, BBC.co.uk, March 2011)

Some forward-thinking neighboring nations, like Japan and South Korea have forged agreements that allow students to take courses and transfer credits between universities in both countries. Another trend across the developed world is the notion of international universities, where courses are taught in English or a language other than the host country's primary language. As part of its globalization efforts, South Korea now offers programs taught all in English at nearly a quarter of its universities. In addition, an increasing number of top universities are opening their doors overseas. Some Middle Eastern nations, such as Oman and the United Arab Emirates already have branch campuses of several American and European universities. In its capital Doha, Qatar has an entire 'Education City', boasting eight international university campuses — six American, one UK, and one French — all in just one 14 square kilometer area.

[5] Better universities serve to boost a nation's economy by bringing in more international students. However, the aim isn't purely financial. Many nations are also looking to universities as a tool to help them gain prestige and recognition on the world stage. The hope is that by positioning universities as international magnets for talent, nations will attract top-level students and researchers and secure their future as innovators in areas such as science, technology, and art.

▪ PATH TO A MORE PEACEFUL TOMORROW?

[6] In addition to the growing numbers of students studying internationally, it is important to note the role of new technology. Contrary to past limitations, today's laptop toting students literally have the world at their fingertips. They can enter a virtual campus with few or no international or intellectual boundaries. They can enroll in online courses with classmates from various other countries, download lectures from international universities, and network with students, professors and prospective employers on the other side of the world.

[7] As these global education trends continue to create wonderful opportunities for international networking in the academic arena, we can be hopeful that this spirit of global cooperation will result in lasting positive effects on foreign relations in the long term.

ACADEMIC KEYWORDS

crisis	(n)	/ˈkraɪsɪs/
notion	(n)	/ˈnəʊʃ(ə)n/
recent	(adj)	/ˈriːsənt/

THINK ABOUT:
economy
foreign relations
jobs and business
languages

Developing critical thinking

Discuss these questions in a group.

1 What do you think are the pros and cons of going to university in another country? What about attending an all-English (or other language) university in your own country?

2 What effects do you think the globalization of education may have on the world in the future?

READING 2 Career trends

Before you read

1 Which methods do you think are most useful for finding a job? Rank them according to their usefulness for finding a job. (1= least useful and 6 = most useful).

- Business or professional networking websites
- Newspaper listings
- Job postings on a company's website
- Social networking websites (Facebook, Twitter)
- Referral from someone you know at a company
- University career center

Global reading

Read *Career trends*. Then answer the questions.

1 What type of document is it? What is its purpose?
2 Who might find the information useful?
3 According to the article, what is changing for job seekers? What about for employers?
4 What do you think the three main points to remember are from the article?

Close reading

READING STATISTICAL DATA

For academic assignments and on some standardized tests, you may need to be able to read and interpret this information, or summarize it in writing.

Focus on key information and trends shown in charts and graphs by asking yourself questions, for example:

- Which is the largest/smallest/tallest/shortest bar, section, or line?
- How do the bars/lines/sections compare to each other?
- How does the trend change over time? At what point did it change?
- Which point shows the average number?
- What overall pattern does the graph or chart show?
- Look for additional useful information outside the actual chart, such as statements or summary information.

Use the information in the charts to answer these questions.

1 What two activities are job seekers most likely to use professional networking sites for?
2 Which activity are they least likely to use a social network for?
3 What are the two least common ways that companies find new hires?
4 What is the most effective way for applicants to connect with a company?
5 Which career sectors saw the most job growth in the past month?
6 How does the growth of education jobs compare to that of health and medical jobs?

ACADEMIC KEYWORDS

contrary to (adj) /ˈkɑnˌtreri tə/
primary (adj) /ˈpraɪm(ə)ri/
summarize (v) /ˈsʌməˌraɪz/

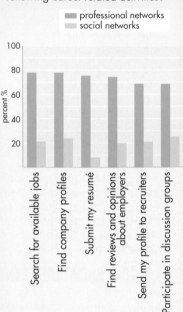

Chart 1 Online job search preferences

Where would you prefer to do the following career-related activities?

- professional networks
- social networks

(bar chart, percent %, axis marked 20, 40, 60, 80, 100)

Categories:
Search for available jobs
Find company profiles
Submit my resumé
Find reviews and opinions about employers
Send my profile to recruiters
Participate in discussion groups

Students indicate that they want to interact with employers on professional networks.

They are afraid that they might be rejected for the wrong reasons if employers see their personal profiles.

CAREER TRENDS

[1] This paper summarizes the findings of this year's Global Careers Conference, organized by the employment industry think tank, **Career Thought Leaders**. The meeting included 250 career leaders from Canada, the U.S., and the U.K. Discussion topics included innovations and trends impacting global employment, recruiting, hiring, and job search practices.

WHAT'S HAPPENING NOW?

JOB SEARCHING:

[2] Contrary to some past predictions, the traditional résumé is still the basic starting point for any job search. While there has been a surge in the use of online professional profiles and personal Web pages, most employers still prefer a well-crafted, concise résumé, which summarizes the applicant's experience and highlights their most valuable skills. In a flooded job market, 'extras' such as volunteer work, special training, or membership in professional organizations can help get employers' attention and distinguish a candidate from others.

[3] When it comes to making contact with employers, job seekers say they prefer professional networks, such as LinkedIn and Careerbuilder, over social media, such as Facebook. (See Chart 1)

HIRING

[4] Web searches are the primary method employers use to gain knowledge about job candidates. Applicants need to be cautious about their online image and the information they post on social networks, even those with so-called privacy settings.

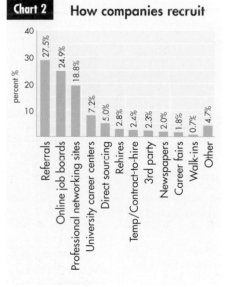

Chart 2 — How companies recruit

Referrals 27.5%, Online job boards 24.9%, Professional networking sites 18.8%, University career centers 7.2%, Direct sourcing 5.0%, Rehires 2.8%, Temp/Contract-to-hire 2.4%, 3rd party 2.3%, Newspapers 2.0%, Career fairs 1.8%, Walk-ins 0.7%, Other 4.7%

[5] Most companies recruit new people through direct referrals to the company or online job boards. (See Chart 2)

CAREER OPPORTUNITIES

[6] The fields of healthcare, technology, and retail remain strong, while the education job market is weak. (See Chart 3) It is estimated that in the coming years the nursing, retail, and customer service sectors will be enjoying the most growth.

WHAT WILL THE FUTURE BRING?

JOB SEARCHING

[7] More applicants will be including high-tech multimedia features, such as videos, and interactive graphics in their application packets. They'll be uploading them onto a professional network site, and providing employers with the link on their résumés. While this is an option for candidates wanting to make an impression, employers from some institutions said they still rely more on the information in the résumé itself.

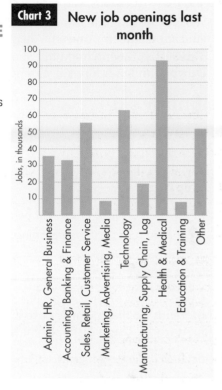

Chart 3 — New job openings last month

Jobs, in thousands

Admin, HR, General Business; Accounting, Banking & Finance; Sales, Retail, Customer Service; Marketing, Advertising, Media; Technology; Manufacturing, Supply Chain, Log; Health & Medical; Education & Training; Other

[8] Employers will be using social networking sites more frequently to both recruit and check out prospective employees. As a consequence, Internet privacy will become of greater concern, as job applicants try to separate their professional and personal profiles.

HIRING

[9] Social networking sites, such as Facebook and Twitter, will likely be providing more services for professional networking. They'll be expanding options for recruiters to post job openings and for job seekers to create professional profiles.

CONCLUSION

[10] In summary, a traditional resume is still the best way to represent your professional accomplishments. Technology, including social media, will continue to play an even larger role in professional networking, so job seekers should make efforts to keep a clean online profile.

Developing critical thinking

1 Discuss these questions in a group.

  1 Which trends described in *Career trends* do you think affect your and your classmates most directly? Do they affect you positively or negatively?

  2 Think of two more points to add to the 'What will the future bring?' section of the document. Share them with the class.

2 Think about the ideas from *Global graduates* and *Career trends* and discuss these questions in a group.

  1 What is the possible impact of new technology on the fields of education and employment? List some pros and cons.

  2 Think of a growing trend in education or employment in your country. Do you think it is a positive trend? Is it likely to continue?

Vocabulary skill

VOCABULARY FOR DESCRIBING TRENDS

There is a special vocabulary for describing upward and downward trends in charts and graphs.

*There has been a **surge** in the numbers of university graduates.* (= going up)

*Service industry jobs will be **declining**.* (= going down)

Read the examples in exercise 1. Note that nearly all the words can be used as both a noun and a verb.

1 What trends do these words describe? Write *U* (upward) or *D* (downward). Use a dictionary if needed.

1	decline ___	5	grow ___	9	soar ___
2	decrease ___	6	increase ___	10	spike ___
3	dip ___	7	plunge ___		
4	dive ___	8	skyrocket ___		

2 Choose the correct information to describe each of the charts on the right.

Chart 1 Retail sales **spiked / decreased** in June and then **rose / dipped** in July. They remained steady until December, when they **skyrocketed / plunged**.

Chart 2 After a **decline / rise** over the past year, the number of international students is predicted to **decline / grow** next year. The numbers will be continuing to **increase / fall** through the year 2020.

Chart 3 There will be an overall **rise / decline** in technology jobs in the beginning of the year. The number of new jobs will **dive / peak** in August. However, they will begin **rising / dipping** again in October.

Chart 4 The number of students using public transportation has **surged / declined** since last year. There was also a **rise / decline** in bicycle use, as well as **an increase / a fall** in students walking to campus.

3 Look at the charts in *Career trends*. Write a sentence about each one, using words and phrases from exercise 1.

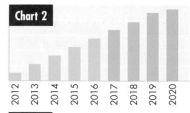

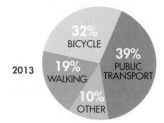

THINK ABOUT:

achievement	distractions
boys vs. girls	efficiency
concentration	independence
cost	motivation

WRITING A report on a current trend

You are going to learn about qualifying statistical data and using the future progressive. You are then going to write a report on a trend affecting your school, city, town, or country.

Writing skill

QUALIFYING STATISTICAL DATA

In addition to nouns and verbs for describing upward and downward trends, the following words can help you describe statistics and trends more accurately.

<u>Adjectives/Adverbs</u>

rapid / rapidly   steep / steeply

sharp / sharply   sudden / suddenly

slight / slightly

*A **sudden surge** in gasoline prices caused airfares to rise.*

*The number of education jobs **dipped slightly** last year.*

<u>Other expressions</u>

*Housing costs will continue to **fluctuate** in this unstable economy. (change back and forth)*

*University tuition costs will **remain steady** for the next few years. (stay the same)*

Complete the sentences about the charts. Use expressions for describing trends and include adjectives and adverbs from the Writing skills box.

a	b	c

Chart a

1 Gas prices will _____ for several months and then will begin to _____.

2 Economic growth will _____ for the next few months. However there will be a _____ after that.

Chart b

1 Computer prices will _____ over the past year. They will _____ in the middle of the year but will _____ after that.

2 There was a _____ in the number of people who say they recycle. The numbers _____ in the summer and have _____ since then.

Chart c

1 Tablet computer sales _____ last month. However, there was a _____ when the school year started, and sales still _____.

2 There was a _____ in the number of students majoring in English over the past few years. Then numbers _____ last year, and they continue to _____.

Grammar

THE FUTURE PROGRESSIVE

The future progressive is used to describe actions that will continue in the future.

Form	Example
Will + be + -ing	*More and more people **will be using** tablet computers and therefore buying more e-books.*

This tense is particularly useful for making predictions and describing future trends.

1 Complete these excerpts from *Career trends* with the future progressive form of the verbs in the box. Then go back to the end of the article on page 101 to check your answers.

> expand   include   provide   upload   use

1 More applicants _____ high-tech multimedia features, such as videos and interactive graphics in their application packets.

2 They _____ them onto a professional network site and providing employers with the link on their résumés.

3 Employers _____ social networking sites more frequently to both recruit and check out prospective employees.

4 Social networking sites, such as Facebook and Twitter, _____ more services for professional networking.

5 They _____ options for recruiters to post job openings and for job seekers to create professional profiles.

2 Work with a partner. Ask and answer these questions.

1 Where do you think you will be living in ten years? What will you be doing?

2 Which job sectors do you think will be growing in your country over the next five to ten years?

3 What other job sectors do you think will be emerging in the future?

4 How do you think people will be traveling in 2050? How will they be communicating?

WRITING TASK

Write a report on a trend affecting a group of people (e.g. people in your class, school, neighborhood, city, town, or country), and make predictions for the future.

Audience:	classmates/peers
Context:	a survey and report on a current trend
Purpose:	to make predictions based on analysis of statistical information and trends

BRAINSTORM

1 Choose one of these topics.

- Communication
- The economy
- Education
- Employment
- The environment
- Housing
- Technology
- Transportation

2 Think about an aspect of your topic that has changed or is changing. Make some notes about the change and any reasons you can think of for the change.

PLAN

Gather information and statistical data about your topic. You can use:

- Interviews
- Surveys and questionnaires
- Newspaper articles
- Books or magazines
- The Internet
- Public records (e.g. at the city library or at City Hall)

WRITE

1 Write a one-page report that describes the trend and its effects in detail. Include one or two charts, graphs, or tables to express the statistical data you found in your report.

2 Write a conclusion to your report that gives your prediction for how the trend will continue in the future. Use the future progressive when possible.

SHARE

Exchange papers with a partner. Do you understand the report? Are the explanations of the graphs or charts clear? Is there any information that could be clearer? Do the predications for the future use the future progressive correctly?

REWRITE AND EDIT

Consider your partner's comments and rewrite your report.

Developing a portfolio

by Stella Cottrell

What is the purpose of a portfolio?

A portfolio has several uses:

- it keeps related documents together
- it helps the process of reflection
- it gives the process of self-evaluation and personal development a higher focus in your life
- in some professions, you can take it to job interviews
- it can hold relevant examples and information for when you need them, such as when applying for work placements, work or other courses.

Do you have to keep a portfolio?

A portfolio may be compulsory for your course. However, even if you don't *have* to keep a portfolio, you will probably find it *helpful* to do so to organize your thinking about what you need to do, and to monitor your progress.

What to put in your portfolio

Checking and updating your portfolio

Update your portfolio regularly — at least once or twice a year, and whenever you achieve something new. Re-reading or rewording what you have written may refocus your energies.

7 Your résumé (A careers adviser can help you to compile this.).

1 Full contents list for each section.

2 Self-evaluation and profile sheets, planners and action plans.

3 A profile of vocational and technical skills you have developed.

4 An up-to-date list of courses and training.

5 Certificates (exams, courses, achievements, etc.).

6 An up-to-date list of your work experience, with the dates, addresses of employers, brief job descriptions, your main responsibilities, skills or qualities you demonstrated, and what you learned from doing that work.

8 Your ideas about where you would like to be in seven years' time, and what you need to do to achieve this goal.

9 Examples of your work and interests, if relevant — but without breaking any rules regarding confidentiality. Examples include a copy of a report undertaken during a work placement, slides of your artwork, or a copy of an article you wrote for a student magazine.

10 A personal statement, which should include details of your long- and short-term objectives, what you have done towards achieving them so far, and a summary of your skills and qualities with supporting examples.

11 Degree or course certificates, transcript.

PALGRAVE
STUDY SKILLS

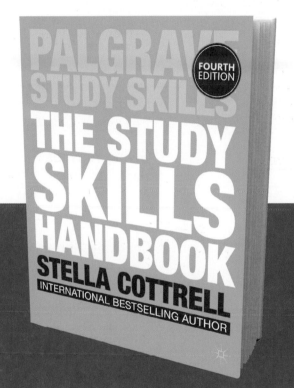
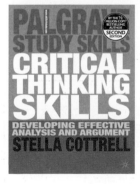
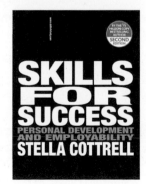

The phrases below give common ways of expressing useful functions.
Use them to help you as you're completing the *Discussion points* and
Developing critical thinking activities.

Asking for clarification

Sorry, can you explain that some more?
Could you say that another way?
When you say …, do you mean …?
Sorry, I don't follow that.
What do you mean?

Asking for repetition

Could you repeat that, please?
I'm sorry, I didn't catch that.
Could you say that again?

When you don't know the meaning of a word

What does … mean?
Sorry, I'm not sure what … means.

Working with a partner

Would you like to start?
Shall I go first?
Shall we do this one first?
Where do you want to begin?

Giving opinions

I think that …
It seems to me that …
In my opinion …
As I see it …

Agreeing and disagreeing

I know what you mean.
That's true.
You have a point there.
Yes. I see what you're saying, but …
I understand your point, but …
I don't think that's true.

Asking for opinions

Do you think …?
Do you feel …?
What do you think about …?
How about you, Jennifer? What do you think?
What about you?
Does anyone have any other ideas?
Do you have any thoughts on this?

Asking for more information

In what way?
Why do you think that?
Can you give an example?

Not giving a strong preference

It doesn't matter to me.
I don't really have a strong preference.
I've never really thought about that.
Either is fine.

Expressing interest

I'd like to hear more about that.
That sounds interesting.
How interesting!
Tell me more about that.

Giving reasons

This is … because …
This has to be … because …
I think … because …

Checking understanding

Do you know what I mean?
Do you see what I'm saying?
Are you following me?

Putting things in order

This needs to come first because …
I think this is the most/least important because …
For me, this is the most/least relevant because …

Preventing interruptions

Excuse me, I wasn't finished.
If I could just finish what I was saying…
Let me just finish this, please.
I haven't finished my thought/sentence.

Buying time

Let me think about that for a moment.
Let me gather my thoughts.
Just a minute. I need to think about that.

Clarifying

That's not exactly what I meant.
Sorry, I wasn't clear. Let me put it another way.
That isn't what I was trying to say.

Writing task peer review checklist

Use the checklist below as you read over your partner's work.

PROCESS WRITING CHECKLIST

1 Does the composition have these things:

☐ a title

☐ paragraph indents

☐ double spacing

☐ proper margins

2 How many paragraphs are there?

3 <u>Underline</u> the topic sentence in each paragraph. (If you can't find the topic sentence in any paragraphs, write the numbers of those paragraphs here.) _____

4 Write any target vocabulary from the unit here: _____

5 Highlight any target grammar from the unit.

6 Draw a star (*) by one or two sentences that you especially liked.

7 Write the thesis statement here if there is one: _____

8 Write one question about the content/ideas of the composition for the author:

_____

Reviewers

The publishers would like to thank the following for their thoughtful insights and perceptive comments during the development of the material:

Belgium
Sylviane Granger, at CECL, University of Louvain
Magali Paquot

Egypt
Dr Gaber Khalil, AUC, Cairo

Germany
John Nixon at Universität Stuttgart

Japan
Robert Morton at Chuo University
Lesley Burda Ito

Oman
Mutaz Abumuaath at Nizwa College of Technology, Nizwa

Qatar
Jane Hoelker at Qatar University, Foundation English

Russia
Tatyana Gromoglasova at the Siberian Institute of Management, Novosibirsk

Saudi Arabia
Dr Mohammed Al-Ahaydib and Dr Mohammed Hamdan at Imam Muhammad Ibn Saud University
Dr William Frawley, Education Experts
Heidi Omara

South Korea
Yoonji Kim, and Da Young Song at the Konkuk University Language Institute
Jina Kwon at Seoul National University

Taiwan
Laura Wang at Chung Yuan Christian University
Regina Jan at Lunghwa University of Science and Technology
Kitty Chu, Jessie Huang, Jenny Jen, and Wenyau Keng at the National Central University, Language Center
Sandrine Ting at the Department of Applied Foreign Language, St. John's University

Thailand
Wanpen Chaikitmongkol, Jindarat De Vleeschauwer, and Sonhsi Wichaidit at the English Division, Department of Western Languages and Humanities, Chiang Mai University

Turkey
Merve Oflaz at Bahcesehir University
Şahika Özkan-Tuğba Kın-Yadigar Aslan, Didem Gümüşlüoğlu, Meltem Sarandal, and Sibel Weeks at Doğuş University, İstanbul
Sevil Altikulaçoğlu, Sühendan Semine Er, Şerife Ersöz, Fatma Ünveren Gürocak at Gazi University
Deniz Ateşok at Istanbul Bilgi University
Ebru Yamaç at Maltepe University,
Aybike Oğuz at Özyeğin University

United Arab Emirates
Paul Barney, Doug Henderson, and Danielle Norris at Higher Colleges of Technology, Al Ain

United Kingdom
Nick Hillman at Anglia Ruskin University
Heather Abel and Richard Hillman at Bell London
Edward Bressan, Sara Hannam, and Stacey Hughes at Oxford Brookes University
Fiodhna Gardiner-Hyland at University of Limerick
Sally Morris, Ian Pople, and Simon Raw at University of Manchester
Averil Bolser and Peter Leverai at University of Nottingham, Ningbo
Jonathan Hadley

United States
Gail Schafers at Fontbonne Univeristy
Carole Mawson at Stanford University
Denise Mussman at University of Missouri
Abby Brown

Macmillan Education
Between Towns Road, Oxford OX4 3PP
A division of Macmillan Publishers Limited
Companies and representatives throughout the world

ISBN 978-0-230-42997-0

Designed by emc design ltd
Illustrated by emc design ltd
Cover design by emc design ltd
Cover illustration/photograph by Thinkstock/iStockphoto
Picture research by Emily Taylor

The Academic Keyword List (AKL) was designed by Magali Paquot at
the Centre for English Corpus Linguistics, Université catholique de
Louvain (Belgium) within the framework of a research project led by
Professor Sylviane Granger.

http://www.uclouvain.be/en-372126.html

Authors' acknowledgements:

Jennifer Bixby
My appreciation and thanks go to the team at Macmillan Education,
to my Skillful colleagues, to Dorothy Zemach, and especially to my
co-author, Jaimie Scanlon. For their support, my thanks to my family-
Ken, Emily, and Claire. I dedicate this book to my parents, WK and BJ
Bixby, who instilled in me a love of reading and writing.

Jaimie Scanlon
Thank you to Morris, Rei and Senji for providing ideas,
encouragement and an unlimited supply of laughter throughout the
writing of this book. Thanks also to my parents, Tom and Laurie
Scanlon for always being proud of me.

In addition, I would like to express my appreciation to my co-author,
Jenny Bixby, for her advice and camaraderie, to Dorothy Zemach for
her years of mentorship, as well as to the Macmillan Education team
for their support and collaboration.

The author and publishers would like to thank the following for permission to reproduce their images:

Alamy/Nigel Cattlin p55(moth), Alamy/Anna Colls p74, Alamy/
Corfield p61(br), Alamy/David R. Frazier p75, Alamy/Mary Evans
Picture Library p89, Alamy/Photoshot Holdings Ltd p51(tr), Alamy/
Kevin Schafer p91, Alamy/SCPhotos p105, Alamy/View Pictures Ltd
p18, Alamy/Zoonar GmbH p41(cr);
AP/Press Association Images p68;
Axiom/Philip Lee Harvey p37;
Corbis pp47, 81, Corbis/Amana Images p64, Corbis/Ingo Arndt/
Minden Pictures p55(butterfly), Corbis/Matthew Ashton/AMA p7,
Corbis/Astock p17, Corbis/Blend Images LLC pp96, 97, Corbis/
Ashley Cooper p44, Corbis/Creativ Studio Heinemann p66, Corbis/

Stephen Dalton/Minden Pictures p48(tr), Corbis/Digital Art p58,
Corbis/Michael Durham/Minden Pictures p49(tr), Corbis/David
Ebener/dpa p27, Corbis/Peter M. Fisher p35, Corbis/Yves Gellie
p20(tr), Corbis/Hannes Hepp p31, Corbis/Jon Hicks p93, Corbis/
Image Source pp15(tr), 82, Corbis/Helen King p59, Corbis/Kirn
Vintage Stock p33, Corbis/Jacob Maentz p69(ocean), Corbis/Matthias
Kulka p56, Corbis/Yva Momatiuk and John Eastcott p55(salmon),
Corbis/Moodboard p11, Corbis/Ocean p86, Corbis/Tim Pannell
p15(cr), Corbis/Nigel Pavitt/John Warburton-Lee Photography Ltd
p87, Corbis/Martin Puddy p29, Corbis/Reuters p50, Corbis/Jens
Rotzsche/ImageZoo p9(bl), Corbis/Daniel Schoenen/Imagebroker
p61(tr), Corbis/Visuals Unlimited p55(mussel), Corbis/Bernd Vogel
p12, Corbis/Hugo Willcox/Minden Pictures p48(br);
FotoLibra/John Cleare p88, FotoLibra/Mark Ferguson p70;
Getty Images/All Canada Images p39, Getty Images/Alistair Baker
p26, Getty Images/Susan Barr p65, Getty Images/Bridgeman Art
Library p52, Getty Images/Jim Doberman p51(background), Getty
Images/Mark Douet p22, Getty Images/Chad Ehlers p67, Getty
Images/Flickr RF pp49(tl), 83, 84, Getty Images/Flickr Select p23,
Getty Images/Fotosearch RF p54, Getty Images/Fuse p9(tl), Getty
Images/Glowimages p57, Getty Images/Terry Husebye p95, Getty
Images/Iconica p71, Getty Images/Image Source p85, Getty Images/
Ron Krisel p9(cl), Getty Images/Bruce Laurance p15(br), Getty
Images/Frans Lemmens p10, Getty Images/MIXA p41(tm), Getty
Images/Dave Porter p43, Getty Images/Baerbel Schmidt p99, Getty
Images/Sot p103, Getty Images/Tetra Images p104, Getty Images/
Pawel Toczynski p25, Getty Images/Vetta pp45, 77, Getty Images/
Barbara Zanon p20(br);
Houghton Mifflin Harcourt Publishing Company/Adrift: Seventy-
six Days Lost at Sea by Steven Callahan (Boston: Mariner Books,
2002) p69;
Image Source p18;
Link Up/Link Up 'http://blog.linkup.com/2011/04/05/jobs-on-
company-websites-increase-substantially-in-march' p101;
Macmillan Australia p55(whale);
Moving Windmills Project Ltd c/o Fogel Neale Partners LLC p79;
OECD/Based on data from OECD (2011), Education at a Glance
2011: Highlights, OECD Publishing. http://dx.doi.org/10.1787/
eag_highlights-2011-en p98;
Rex Features/ITV p72;
Potentialpark Group/'Social Media Vs Professional Networks'
(University Report – Europe – Switzerland 2011 p100.

The author(s) and publishers are grateful for permission to reprint the
following copyright material:

Material from 'The Study Skills Handbook' by author Stella Cottrell,
copyright © Stella Cottrell 1999, 2003 & 2008, first published by
Palgrave Macmillan, reproduced with permission of the publisher.

Printed and bound in Thailand

2017 2016 2015 2014 2013
10 9 8 7 6 5 4 3 2 1

Recommended minimum system requirements for the *Skillful* Digibook

Windows

	Windows XP SP3	Vista	Windows 7 & 8
CPU Speed	Core 2 Duo, 2.53 GHz	Core 2 Duo, 2.53 GHz	Core 2 Duo, 2.93 GHz
Browser	Explorer 8 & 9, Firefox, and Chrome		

Macintosh OS

	10.6	10.7	10.8
CPU Speed	Core 2 Duo – 1.83 GHz	Core 2 Duo – 1.83 GHz	Core 2 Duo – 1.83 GHz
Browser	Safari		

Additional recommended minimum system requirements

- Hard Disk (offline version only): Minimum 1 GB free on the install drive and minimum 2 GB free on the system drive.
- Free RAM: 500 MB
- Display: 1024 x 768 pixels, 32-bit colour
- Add-ins: Flash Player 10.1
- Broadband connection: For Authentication/Registration/Download (offline version only)/Updates

Please visit help.macmillan.com for technical support

This software is licensed for use by one user and can be installed on a maximum of one machine.

Product Activation

1 Type *www.skillfuldigibooks.com* into your Internet browser.

2 Click "Enter your token details"

3 You need your access token code, printed on the next page.

4 Type your access token code into the box provided.

5 Follow the step-by-step instructions on the screen to help you register and log-in.

6 You can now use your *Skillful* DigiBook.

Your access token code only allows one user to log in, so don't give yours away, and make sure you use it within one year!